GREAT
MOMENTS
IN
FOOTBALL

GREAT MOMENTS IN FOOTBALL

by Howard Liss

COWLES BOOK COMPANY, INC.
NEW YORK

Cowles Book Company, Inc.
A subsidiary of Cowles Communications, Inc.
Published simultaneously in Canada by
   General Publishing Company, Ltd., 30 Lesmill Road,
   Don Mills, Toronto, Ontario
Planned and Produced by the Sayre Ross Company.
Printed in the United States of America
First Edition

CONTENTS

In the Beginning

Princeton vs. Rutgers—
November 6, 1869

In order to qualify as a "great game," a football contest must have certain prerequisites:

a) It must be close and hard-fought, at least part of the time. If one team puts up a struggle for a half or three quarters, and then runs out of gas, that's all right, no matter what the final score is. That is why the 1940 professional football championship game between Chicago and Washington could never be called great or even good. The Bears jumped off to a big lead in the opening period and when the smoke cleared they had won the game, 73–0. Not only wasn't the score close at any time, the Redskins just folded up when the game was out of reach. It was something of an embarrassment . . . to both sides.

b) There should be some element of drama to the game. This can take many forms: tradition, such as that of the annual Army-Navy match, or of the Harvard-Yale yearly scrap; or it can be a grudge game, with one team looking for revenge because of a previous humiliation or upset; even the big upset can count as a great game, because it produces the unexpected victory by the "little guy," a kind of victory so close to American hearts.

c) A great game has great stars participating, and more often than not these outstanding players put on a show that alone is worth the price of admission. It's all right even when they shine in a losing cause.

d) Or, it can be a "first." Take, as an example, the very first football game ever played, between Princeton and Rutgers, way back in 1869. Of course, some purists claim that it bore no more resemblance to modern football than the old ice game of "shinny" did to today's ice hockey. And that's true enough. Still, there had to be a beginning somewhere, and this was as good a one as any. Besides, it was *called* football, which should count for some points in its favor.

Fortunately for football historians, the Rutgers student newspaper, *The Targum*, sent a man to report the action. The following is a verbatim account of the game, as published in The Newark *Sunday News* on September 21, 1969, commemorating the 100th anniversary of the first game.

On Saturday, November 6, Princeton sent 25 picked men to play our 25 a match game of football. The strangers came up in the 10 o'clock train, and brought a good number of backers with them. After dinner and a stroll around the town, during which stroll billiards received a good deal of attention, the crowds began to assemble at the ball ground, which, for the benefit of the ignorant, we would say is a lot about 100 yards wide, extending from College Avenue to Sicard Street. Previous to calling the game, the ground presented an animated picture. Grim-looking players were silently stripping, each one surrounded by sympathizing friends, while around each of the captains was a little crowd, intent upon giving advice, and saying as much as possible. The appearance of the Princeton men was very different from that of our own players. They were almost without exception tall and muscular, while the majority of our 25 are small and light, but possess the merit of being up to much more than they look.

Very few were the preliminaries, and they were quickly agreed upon. The Princeton captain, for some reason or other, gave up every point to our men without contesting one. The only material points were that Princeton gave up "free kicks," whereby a player, when he catches the ball in the air is allowed to kick it without hindrance. On the other hand, our practice of "babying" the ball on the start was discarded, and the ball was mounted, in every instance, by a vigorous "long kick."

Princeton won the toss, and chose the first mount, rather oddly, since it had been agreed to start the ball against the wind. At 3 p.m., the game was called. The Princetonians suffered from making a very bad "mount" or "buck" as they call it, the effects of which were not remedied before the sides closed, and after a brief struggle, Rutgers drove it home, and won, amid great applause from the crowd. The sides were changed, Rutgers started the ball, and after a somewhat longer fight, Princeton made it a tie by a well-directed kick, from a gentleman whose name we don't know, but who did the best kicking on the Princeton side.

To describe the varying fortunes of the match, game by game, would be a waste of labor, for every game was like the one before. There was the same head-long running, wild shouting, and frantic kicking.

In every game the cool goaltenders saved the Rutgers goal half a dozen times; in every game the heavy charger of the Princeton side overthrew everything he came in contact with; and in every game, just when the interest in one of those delightful rushes at the fence was culminating, the persecuted ball would fly off for refuge into the next lot, and produce a cessation of hostilities until, after the invariable "foul," it was put in straight.

Well, at last we won the match, having won the 1st, 3rd, 5th, 6th, 9th and 10th games; leaving Princeton the 2nd, 4th, 7th and 8th. The seventh game would probably have been added to our score, but for one of our players, who, in his ardor, forgot which way he was kicking, a mistake which he fully atoned for afterward.

To sum up, Princeton had the most muscle, but didn't kick very well, and wanted organization. They evidently don't like to kick the ball on the ground. Our men, on the other hand, though comparatively weak, ran well, and kicked well throughout. But their great point was their organization, for which great praise is due to the captain, Leggett, '72. The right men were always in the right places.

After the match, the players had an amicable "feed" together, and at 8 o'clock our guests went home in high good spirits, but thirsting to beat us next time, if they can.

That 100-year-old account was pretty good sportswriting. Fans who are true students of football (are there any other kind?) can see here the beginning of a change from regular soccer, which is centuries old, to football, a youngster by comparison.

True, the ball then was round and not oval as it is

10

today. Also true, the ball was advanced by kicking. And there were soccer-type goaltenders. But a player was permitted to *catch* the ball, and in soccer nobody except the goalie can touch the ball with his hands. Soccer supposedly has little or no actual body contact, while the "scrimmages" of that first Princeton-Rutgers meeting were more like street corner free-for-alls than a game with rules and regulations.

In the Rutgers gymnasium is a plaque giving the names of all the players who participated (Princeton men included). In beautiful, clear typescript it reads, "Here, November 6, 1869, on what was then College Field, took place the First Intercollegiate Football Contest ever held."

That's what they called it. And the Rutgers people should know, because they were there when it happened.

One for the Gipper

Notre Dame vs. Army—
November 11, 1928

Almost every middle-aged movie fan throughout the length and breadth of the United States knows the scene by heart.

The setting: a hospital room. The time: December 14, 1920. The characters: irascible but kindly Knute Rockne, head coach of the Notre Dame football team (played by Pat O'Brien), and the once dashing and daring, but now wasted and wan, George Gipp (played by Ronald Reagan), star of the Notre Dame backfield. Gipp, stricken by a fatal illness, speaks in a slow, painful, wistful whisper: "I've got to go, Rock. . . . It's all right. I'm not afraid. . . . Some time, Rock, when the team's up against it—when things are wrong and the breaks are beating the boys—tell them to go in there with all they've got . . . and win one for the Gipper! I don't know where I'll be then, Rock . . . but I'll know about it . . . and I'll be happy. . . ."

Cut! Print it!

Now, many years after the film was made, it's a full-fledged cliché. People grin broadly when they talk about that pathetic but corny scene—a real tear inducer. It sounds like the writing of a dime-a-dozen Hollywood scripter who batted it out during a coffee break. Yet, although veteran actor Pat O'Brien and California Governor Ronald Reagan made many motion pictures before and after the Rockne epic, that is the one they all remember best, and the "deathbed scene" is the one that stands out.

Oddly enough, Gipp's words weren't invented by a movie writer. According to Rockne's biography, he really said them. Perhaps he wanted Knute to use them some day, for he knew the kind of man the Notre Dame coach was.

As for his playing ability, there is no question that George Gipp was one of the best college backs in America at that time, an authentic triple threat. Even as a freshman he flashed starring form. In a game against Western State Normal in 1916, Gipp drop-kicked a 62-yard field goal, just one yard short of the record. And he kept improving all the time.

It was as a junior that Gipp established his reputation nationally. Playing against Army, he ran and passed and kicked and practically took the West Pointers apart single-handed. He gained 124 yards from scrimmage, ran back kicks for 112 yards and added 96 yards more via passes. Final personal total: 332 yards gained; final score of the game: Notre Dame 27, Army 17.

It should be added that the Gipper was also quite a baseball player. In fact the Chicago Cubs of the National League were interested enough to offer him a contract.

Gipp continued his gridiron heroics in his senior year. But he didn't last out the full season. After the Northwestern game late in November, he complained of dizziness and fever. Aches and ague racked his body. Doctors immediately diagnosed the illness as pneumonia and he was hospitalized.

For weeks his condition fluctuated wildly. At first it seemed that he had passed the crisis and was on the road to recovery, but a day later he suffered a relapse. Three times his illness deepened, and three times Gipp rallied, fighting back with amazing stamina.

It wasn't pneumonia that finally dropped him into eternal sleep, but a strep throat infection. This was two decades before the discovery of such miracle drugs as sulfa and penicillin; the doctors had no way then to fight such germs.

The Rockne-Gipp scene took place just as described. When Gipp passed away, Rockne wept bitter tears, for he truly loved the boy. Indeed, Rockne considered himself a second father to the entire football squad. The affection was always returned.

A few hours before the end, Gipp learned that Walter Camp had selected him for his all-American team. It is said that Gipp died with a faint smile on his lips, and if that sounds contrived—well, so much the worse for the unbelievers, for it happened that way.

George Gipp's death had a shattering effect on the entire Notre Dame student body and faculty, and on all sports fans in general. Sacks of letters and telegrams of sympathy flooded the tiny college in South Bend, Indiana. It was a genuine, spontaneous outpouring of grief. All businesses in Gipp's home town of Larium, Michigan, were closed the day of the funeral. The Notre Dame football squad served as honorary pallbearers.

So the bright young backfield ace was gone, and

ONE FOR THE GIPPER

slowly the memory of him dimmed. Oh, the fans and the sportswriters mentioned his name often enough, and when some promising runner or passer showed up at Notre Dame, he was inevitably compared with Gipp. Still, he didn't quite become the legendary figure of Notre Dame football—that is, on a par with Rockne himself. That came later.

Knute Rockne himself blossomed into America's idea of what a college coach should be—a combination of football tactician, father confessor, and inspirational leader. In part, because of the winning image he established, Notre Dame became everybody's favorite team. They always played to packed stadiums, especially when they came to New York to take on "Brave Old Army Team." The record Rockne established was truly amazing. In his thirteen years as head coach, Notre Dame football teams won 105, lost 12, and tied 5. They scored 2,847 points to the opposition's 667.

But Rockne also had showmanship. Long before anyone else thought of the idea, he put gold-colored pants on his football players. And when the team was in New York, with its large Irish population, Rockne trotted out gorgeous green jerseys for his boys. For years everybody thought the school's colors were green and gold, but they weren't; actually, the team's official colors were gold and blue. But no one knew that, and Rockne wasn't about to tell. So Notre Dame became a kind of "home team" for New York's Irish. Whenever they lost one, the gloom in the Third Avenue pubs was pea-soup thick.

And when they did drop an occasional game, the one who took it hardest was Rockne. He wasn't accustomed to losing. He'd brood and snarl and try to figure out what went wrong. Even a tie game wasn't accept-

15

able. It was win or nothing in Rockne's scheme of things.

On November 10, 1928, the boys from South Bend were in New York again to play Army. And even the most loyal Notre Dame rooter knew in his heart that the beloved Fighting Irish were due for a shellacking. As far as Rockne was concerned, the season was already a disaster. The club had played six games; they'd won four, lost two. The season's opener had been a 12-6 win over Loyola, but then they had absorbed a 22-6 clobbering at the hands of Wisconsin. A 7-0 victory over a weak Navy team was followed by a 13-0 loss to Georgia Tech. The Irish won the next two, a respectable 32-6 triumph over Drake and a squeak-through 9-0 afternoon with a team that had nothing—Penn State.

Army, on the other hand, was undefeated, and rated the best in the East. Part of their success was due to one of West Point's immortals, running back Chris Cagle. Dubbed "The Gray Ghost," Cagle was fast and elusive, but he could also bull his way straight ahead like a runaway truck.

While Rockne couldn't abide any loss, a defeat by Army was almost more than he could bear. So he gave the boys one of his patented pep talks. He gave them the works, with much about the tradition of victory and the meaning of the word "fight" in their Fighting Irish name. Rockne really lit a fire under his kids. They went onto the field raring to play ball.

More than 85,000 fans were shoe-horned into Yankee Stadium (the game had been sold out for months) and watched Notre Dame and the Cadets battle each other to a standstill in the first half.

The only real scoring threat in the two periods was a Notre Dame surge. Army had been stopped deep in

16

its own territory, and Murrel got off a wobbly punt that sailed out on Army's 35. Notre Dame began driving. Fred Collins went off tackle, got clear, and moved to the West Point 16-yard line. Chevigny went for 5, then Collins added 6 more. Army stiffened. Chevigny went nowhere on his next carry, and when Collins tried again he was belted so hard he fumbled. Murrel recovered for Army in the end zone for an automatic touchback. The ball was brought out to the 20, and the teams went at it all over again.

Once again Army couldn't move the ball. Murrel punted and the Irish went back to the 35 once more. There the attack petered out.

At the halftime intermission, Rockne realized that the club had a good chance to upset the Cadets. Nobody had figured Army to go through two periods against Notre Dame without scoring a few times; so far they'd been shut out. Rock was an astute judge of his men. Another pep talk wouldn't quite do the job. He needed something different. . . .

Perhaps the idea just slipped into his head in a moment of inspiration. Maybe he had been saving it for just such an occasion. No matter how it happened, Rockne didn't merely give out with a lot of fighting words. Instead, his voice soft and almost musing, he began to tell about the last hours of George Gipp.

The locker room was stilled as Rockne came to Gipp's dying words: "When the breaks are beating the boys . . . tell them to win one for the Gipper. . . ."

It was a determined band of Fighting Irish that met the Cadets in the second half. However, Army was just as aroused, and Chris Cagle couldn't be stopped forever. It was Cagle who got the Army attack moving.

17

From his own 28, Cagle slashed through tackle to the 47. On the next play he dropped back, waited for his right end, Messinger, to get free, and fed him the ball, good for 39 yards. It was Cagle, Murrel, and Cagle again to the 4. Cagle took it to the 1-yard line. Murrel struck into the line but was stopped. His number was called again and this time he took it in. The extra point was added. Army led, 7-0.

Notre Dame couldn't get very far with the kickoff, but neither could Army. On the exchange of punts, the Irish came up with the ball on their own 47.

It was a 15-yard penalty that really got the visitors moving. Then Fred Collins made 12 in two carries, and after Chevigny failed to gain, Collins made 12 more. Four plays later they were on Army's 1-yard line, first and goal. The Cadets dug in. Chevigny lost 3, then got back 2 of the lost yards on his next try. Collins bulled ahead to the 1. Chevigny took it across.

The Irish missed the tie as three aroused Cadet linemen broke through and smothered the kick. Army led, 7-6.

Once again the West Point squad was stopped by the fired-up Notre Dame line, and then the backfield went to work again. Chevigny made 15 on three plunges up the middle. This was a "bread-and-butter" series Notre Dame had figured wouldn't work. But when Army kept stopping the cross bucks and the reverses, Rockne's boys had nowhere else to go on the ground except off tackle or through center. Surprisingly, the power smashes were eating up the yardage.

Still they couldn't score again. Notre Dame had a first-and-10 on the Army 37 when the Cadets stopped the drive. Frank Carideo's field-goal attempt fell short and Army still clung to that slender single-point edge. But they couldn't advance the ball either. In fact, the charging Irish line shoved them back a bit. Forced to punt, they messed up that play, too. Notre Dame took over on the 46.

Time was running out on the Irish. Probably another team would have taken to the air immediately, but Rock's boys figured that the straight-ahead plays might work just as well. And they did! Carideo went for 10, Chevigny for 16, and three more line smashes netted 14 hard-won yards. They were on Army's 16 as the Corps of Cadets exhorted their team to hold on, the Irish rooters urging their boys on equally as hard.

The next play produced a groan from the stands and a 16-yard loss for the South Bend team as the snap from center went wild. By the time it was chased down and recovered, the dazed Irish were back on the 32. They looked demoralized, as though their momentum was gone.

Knute Rockne always seemed to find the right man for the right play whenever he needed one badly enough. He looked down the bench and saw a lot of anxious faces, all silently pleading to get into the ball game. He beckoned to an unheralded sub named Johnny O'Brien and sent him in to replace the left end. The kid brought a play with him.

Right halfback Johnny Niemiec took the snap from center, and this time it was good. He dropped back to pass, and waited patiently as the Cadet forward wall surged in. At the last moment Niemiec let it fly. Johnny O'Brien slanted over from his left end position toward the right corner of the end zone. He stopped on the goal line—and there was the ball. Clutching it in his arms, he took one step and fell back into pay dirt. He rose, flipped the ball to the referee, and ran off the field, his feet hardly touching the turf. He hadn't been in the game at all before that play—and he didn't go back into the game after it, either!

The Irish missed the conversion, but now they led, 12–7.

The play that followed gave every loyal rooter of Notre Dame football teams a case of cardiac arrest: Chris Cagle took the kickoff on his own 5-yard line, and he zigged and zagged and ran over tacklers. Cagle galloped for 60 yards before the man who had kicked off—the last Notre Dame player between Cagle and the end zone—brought him down.

As the final seconds slipped away, the courageous Black Knights of the Army team unleashed a savage attack. They bit off 15 yards, and 10 yards, and 9 yards, all the way to the 1-yard line as frantic Irish fans screamed themselves hoarse.

And that was where the game ended. Time ran out before the Cadets could get off just one more play that might have won the game for them.

It was an upset all right, but for a while nobody could figure out what had happened. Had Army been overconfident? Had they taken a supposedly mediocre Notre Dame team too lightly? Or had the Fighting Irish suddenly found the right combination and unlocked the door to victory?

Knute Rockne told everybody that his boys had the ability all the time. He had merely been waiting for the backfield to jell, and when it did, everything fell into place. Army was the victim of a new and rejuvenated Notre Dame team. It was that simple.

But when the knowledgeable people learned of Rockne's locker-room speech, they realized what had happened. Once again the old Rockne magic had worked its spell. Those kids had "won one for the Gipper," but had had to play over their heads to do it.

The loyal Irish fans weren't buying that. Of course Rockne could inspire his team to the heights—that was nothing new—but surely it took more than fighting spirit to stop Army's juggernaut. Notre Dame was the better team.

The Irish played their next game against Carnegie Tech. The contest was held at South Bend. Notre Dame hadn't lost a home game since 1908, and Tech wasn't so special.

The final score: Carnegie Tech 27, Notre Dame 7!

The Great Indian Uprising

Dartmouth vs. Yale—
October 31, 1931

If by chance you ever run across a Yale alumnus, class of 1931, you could make him a very happy man just by asking him to talk about Albie Booth. But you also must expect him to launch into a marathon dissertation on the fine points of football, punctuated by such phrases as "good old Albie," or "the greatest ever," or even "they don't make that kind of player any more." And he'd be absolutely right.

And should you meet a Dartmouth alumnus of the same era, try sounding him out on Bill Morton and Bill McCall. You'll see the quick gleam in his eye, sense the hard gulp swallowing a rising lump in his throat, and hear a torrent of words like "magnificent," or "nobody better," or even "what a pair they were!" And he'd be right too.

Not that either Dartmouth's or Yale's football team was so outstanding that year. In fact, when they clashed that memorable afternoon four decades ago both had already tasted defeat. Dartmouth had earlier lost to Columbia

22

and Yale had been beaten by Georgia and managed to tie Army. But both clubs had also won a few, and it was possible to evaluate them fairly accurately. Yale had the better team. Any outfit which had Albie Booth cavorting in the backfield always rated as a threat; and the Yale line was pretty good, by Ivy League or any other standards. Dartmouth had a stickout passer in quarterback Bill Morton, and Bill McCall, also in the backfield, was one of his best targets. The Dartmouth running game was nothing to speak of, but the aerial attack was solid. Yale could advance the ball equally well by land and air.

Evidently Dartmouth was worried about the outcome of the Yale game, because a week before they clashed, while the Big Green was meeting and beating Lebanon Valley by a score of 20-6, quarterback Bill Morton and a couple of the Hanover coaches were in New Haven scouting the Yale-Army game. What they saw couldn't have made them happy. Not only did Old Eli hold Army to a single touchdown, but Bud Parker gained a tie for Yale with a dazzling 88-yard touchdown run. Dartmouth would have to keep an eye on Parker as well as one on Booth.

And the Dartmouth Indians had another good reason for concern. There was something else working against them, something intangible: the old Yale Bowl jinx. Since 1884, New Haven had been hard luck for Dartmouth. The previous year, when they'd had a good chance to win, the Indians had managed to eke out a tie. Small wonder then that every player on the Dartmouth team—regulars and substitutes alike—went into the ballgame equipped with football pads, a helmet, moleskin pants, a jersey, cleats—and a rabbit's foot!

The first period of the game was surprisingly quiet.

Most of the fifteen minutes was spent in Yale territory, but neither team broke the ice. Dartmouth kept threatening to score, but just when they got rolling, the Eli Bulldogs shoved them back. Late in the quarter Dartmouth drove inside the Yale 20 but stalled there as time ran out.

On the first play of the second period Bill Morton booted a field goal to make the score Indians 3, Bulldogs 0. And that seemed to open the gates, for the rest of the half turned out to be one of the wildest in Ivy League history!

Dartmouth's lead lasted exactly one play. Albie Booth took the kickoff on his own 6-yard line. He raced up the middle, cut over to the sidelines, sidestepped one tackler, broke away from another, and breezed into pay dirt. It was a 94-yard beauty. The kick was no good. Score: Yale 6, Dartmouth 3.

That score remained on the board for just a minute. Bill Morton threw one over the middle, but Albie Booth picked it off and returned it to midfield (players were expected to go both ways, offensive and defensive, in those days). After that it took two plays for the Bulldogs to score. Booth passed to his right end, Herster Barres, down to the 22. Then right halfback Kay Todd flipped one to Booth along the sidelines, and little Albie went in for his second touchdown. Once more the extra point was missed. Yale 12, Dartmouth 3.

Those numbers didn't last long either. Dartmouth couldn't go all the way, and Yale took over in its own territory. After that the name of the game was Albie Booth, as Eli's backfield ace kept jabbing away at the Indians' line. Then, from his own 46, Booth took the snap, went toward the right sideline and turned the corner. He bolted away, and halfway home picked up a key block from his right end, Johnny Sargeant—who wiped out the Dartmouth safety man. Booth practically walked across the goal. And, without blinking an eye, he drop-kicked the extra point: Yale 19, Dartmouth 3. And the flashy little runner led the regulars off the field to give the subs a chance to earn their letters.

Dartmouth brought the kickoff back to its 25-yard line. Now there was no time for finesse, for fancy reverses, or for power runs. The Indians couldn't crack through the Yale line anyway. So they sprang a play they'd been practicing all week. Bill McCall came out of the backfield and circled around. Bill Morton flipped the ball to him. McCall outran everybody into the end zone. The extra point was made. Yale 19, Dartmouth 10.

Perhaps, in other circumstances, the subs might have been pulled and the regulars sent in. But Yale was hip deep in good reserves, and the replacements stayed where they were. This paid off. Yale moved the ball quickly and far, with Bob Lassiter making a 48-yard run. Clem Williamson lugged the leather across. One more point was tacked on via the conversion route. Now it was Yale 26, Dartmouth 10. The gun sounded, mercifully ending the half.

It had been a peculiar half. The first quarter had been scoreless, while the second had produced a total of 36 points, including five touchdowns, three conversions, and one field goal. Albie Booth had scored three of those TDs. The Bulldogs were up, confident; the Indians looked totally demoralized. Even the Yale substitutes could score on them with impunity.

Perhaps things had to get worse before they could get better, or maybe Yale still had momentum carried over from the glorious first half; but no matter what the reason, in the third quarter Old Eli went back to its scoring ways. Taking over on their own 43, Yale drove to another score, with Bob Lassiter passing to Herster Barres for the touchdown. Now it was 33-10, Yale. Some Yale fans talked lightheartedly about leaving early because they couldn't stand to see Dartmouth humiliated.

The kickoff sailed out to Bill McCall, who fielded it on his own 8-yard line. Like a sprinter shooting off the starting blocks, McCall cut diagonally to the sideline, and then just turned on the heat. Nobody had a clean shot at him, and McCall went over the last chalk stripe scarcely breathing hard. Bill Morton, his sidekick, put the ball through the uprights. Yale 33, Dartmouth 17.

McCall's long run seemed to trigger a spark of hope in Dartmouth players. Maybe they weren't as bad as the score indicated. Now, if they could just keep Yale from scoring. . . .

That they did. And when the Blues were halted, Bud Parker went back to punt. Perhaps he thought there was plenty of time to get the ball away, for Parker took his time, turning the ball over in his hands in order to hold it just right before applying his toe. That was his mistake. Right end Roger Donner came tearing in and threw himself in front of the booted ball. It bounded off his chest and back toward the Yale goal line. Without breaking stride Donner took out after it, scooped up the ball and lumbered across the last chalk mark. Once again the conversion was good. Score: Yale 33, Dartmouth 24. And that was how the quarter ended.

Now it was Yale's turn to feel the rising tide of panic. That nine-point lead looked awfully shaky. The breaks were starting to go Dartmouth's way. It was time for the regulars to get back into the game. That included Albie Booth.

Yale had the ball. Booth carried and made 8 through the line. Dartmouth tightened up, looking for the first-down plunge. Yale decided to cross them up, which was good, solid thinking. The play called for in the huddle was a pass to Booth over the middle.

Lefthanded passer Kay Todd saw Booth break momentarily into the clear and he threw that way. But Bill McCall climbed a ladder and made a one-handed baseball-type catch for the interception. He moved away from the crowd of Yale tacklers and inserted himself into a mob of his own blockers. Only he really didn't need them, because McCall outran everybody else, going 60 yards for the touchdown.

Morton missed the conversion, and the score stood at 33-30. At least that was the *real* score. Somehow, the scoreboard people got their own signals crossed. Maybe they thought Morton's attempts were automatically good. At any rate, the scoreboard showed the numbers as 33-31, Yale leading.

Now that it was almost a brand new ball game, Yale went all out to gain a safer edge. The inspired boys from Hanover held, forcing the Elis to punt. And the Indian uprising continued.

Throughout the game Dartmouth had been relying heavily on short passes behind the line of scrimmage. An end or a backfield player would fake going out, then slip back a couple of yards, turn and take a quick pass. Usually it was good for some yardage. Dartmouth could engineer these plays because they used a peculiar type of single-wing formation. One end, on the strong side, played wide of tackle—a sort of split end. The right halfback would station himself outside the end (today he'd be called a flanker), and another back would line up between the split end and the tackle (nowadays he'd be a slot back).

Dartmouth began to murder Yale again with those quickies. One from Morton to Brister gained 19 yards, another to Bill McCall reaped a reward of 20 more. Now Dartmouth was on Yale's 10-yard line, first and goal. The stands were in a frenzy of excitement, with the Yalies dying a thousand deaths and the Indian rooters exhorting their lads ever onward.

Yale's big line rose to the occasion. A power plunge was stopped cold. A behind-the-lines pass from Morton to Brister *lost* 4 yards. It was third and 14. And the guys from Hanover decided to try for a three-pointer instead of the TD.

For many years, the strategy of that call has been argued all over the Ivy League. Was it because the scoreboard still read 33-31, and Morton thought the field goal would put Dartmouth out in front by a single point? Maybe. But Morton himself had tried for all the extra points, and he knew full well he had missed one try. Simple arithmetic would have given him all the facts. Dartmouth had scored four touchdowns; total, 24 points. Morton himself had kicked one field goal and three conversions; total, 6 points. Added up that came to 30.

Most likely Bill Morton did know the real score. But he had to take several factors into account. Although Dartmouth had the momentum and their fires were stoked pretty high, the boys were getting tired. The ball was in perfect position for a field goal, squarely between the uprights; counting yardage behind the line for spotting the ball, and counting the 10-yard end zone, he'd have to kick about 32 or 33 yards, and that was no problem. But if the next play resulted in a fumble, or if it was turned out toward the sideline to give him a bad angle for a kick, why, there goes the old ball game.

Now, if he did make good on the kick, and if Dartmouth could hold Yale and get the ball back, they'd still have a chance to pull it out. There were still something like four minutes left on the clock. It was just good, sound, percentage football.

So McCall held the ball and Morton kicked it and got his tying field goal. That was how the game ended: a 33-33 tie.

Some newspapers said that regardless of the score Yale was the better team. Probably, but not according to the statistics. True, on the ground it was all Eli. They racked up 276 yards rushing to Dartmouth's 35. In fact, the Indians didn't achieve a single first down on the ground. However, Dartmouth gained 215 yards through the air to Yale's 75, which was a kind of equalizer. The battle between Albie Booth and McCall-Morton had resulted in a standoff.

But Yale had the victory in hand and they let it slip away, and they knew it, too. There was some reshuffling in the backfield, and a sub named Jim Crowley took over for Kay Todd. "Sleepy Jim," as he was known later, in his coaching days, became an instant star. In Yale's next game, against a team from St. Johns of Annapolis, the Bulldogs won, 52-0. Crowley scored five touchdowns!

The Fighting Irish Fight Back

Notre Dame vs. Ohio State—
November 2, 1935

There's something about four years of college that gets into a man's bloodstream. It isn't merely the education or the lasting friendships formed. Perhaps the true reason can be found in the dictionary definition of the phrase *alma mater*: "a school, college, or university at which one has studied, and, usually, from which one has graduated. (Latin: nourishing, i.e. dear, mother.)"

So when Dad graduates from an Ivy League school or a Big Ten school, it's a cinch his sons are expected to attend the old alma mater. Even before modern classroom shortages, before it seemed necessary to try and make sure of a place in college, dear old Dad would enroll his son at Harvard or Wisconsin on the very afternoon the child was born.

Colleges, in turn, usually reciprocate this feeling of togetherness. If there is a spot open on the coaching faculty and there are two applicants for it, who gets the job? Why, the alumnus, of course! And if two equally qualified student hopefuls want the last remaining place in school, who is accepted? Why, the son, or the brother, or the cousin of a graduate.

The Notre Dame team of 1935 was a case in point. The coach was none other than Elmer Layden, one of Knute Rockne's immortal "Four Horsemen." Playing in the backfield was coach Layden's brother, Mike. Also in the backfield was Fred Carideo, cousin of the great Irish backfield ace, Frank Carideo. Neither of these varsity players would have dreamed of attending another school, especially if they intended to play football. Of course, it would have been heresy if Elmer Layden had refused to coach the Notre Dame team. And Layden did a smart job of it, too. Over the years his record averaged out to .783, meaning that his teams won slightly more than three games of every four played, ties not included!

The 1935 Irish had a few others on the roster who weren't half bad. Wayne Millner, who caught footballs when nobody else could get near them, was at end; in the backfield were Bill Shakespeare, sometimes called "the Bard of Staten Island," who could throw a football or run with it, and Andy Pilney, who could throw the ball, kick the ball, run with the ball, and catch the ball. Put them together with Mike Layden and Fred Carideo and there was the makings of a good football team.

But there were better teams than the Irish then, at least on paper. One such was Ohio State, rated as the best in the country. The Buckeye line averaged 210 pounds per man—tremendous weight in those days. The pivot man in the forward wall was their all-American, 220-pound center, Gomer Jones. The backfield boasted a sophomore flash named Joe Williams, who had run wild in every game State played. And under the watchful eye of coach Francis Schmidt, Ohio had learned about multiple type offenses. When they lined up, the opposition didn't know what to expect, for the State team might use a single wing left or right, a short punt formation from which erupted running or passing plays, a split formation sending one of its backs wide, or an unbalanced line right or left.

Did it work? Drake University found out what kind of team Ohio State could be when the Buckeyes trampled over them by a score of 85-7! Even the State subs quit playing hard in the third quarter, but they simply couldn't stop scoring.

Considering the quality of players on both teams, the Notre Dame-Ohio State clash wasn't exactly a mismatch. Both clubs were undefeated, but State was heavily favored. Almost every sportswriter in the nation considered them the number one college team.

Within two minutes of the opening kickoff it seemed that State intended to repeat the Drake score over Notre Dame. The Irish were in possession past midfield and Mike Layden dropped back to pass. His protection evaporated as Gomer Jones and his cohorts brushed aside Notre Dame linemen and blockers alike. Layden's hurried pass was intercepted by Antenucci of State, who promptly lateraled to Frank Boucher, and Boucher followed his blocking down the sidelines for a 65-yard touchdown romp.

The vaunted Irish attack couldn't dent the State line. In fact, the tackling was so savage that Fred Carideo went out of the game early with bruised ribs. But Ohio seemed to encounter little difficulty. With Boucher and Antenucci alternating, the Buckeyes started a 50-yard march, and when they reached the Notre Dame 3-yard line, Joe Williams was sent in. The substitution was almost ludicrous, Ohio was moving so strongly; they didn't seem to require the services of their best runner. As if to prove how easy it was going to be, Williams slid off tackle, spun away from a couple of reaching defenders, and crossed the Irish goal standing up. Now the score was 13-0.

The Buckeyes did no more scoring in the first half, but that appeared to be because they weren't really trying. Notre Dame wasn't going anywhere, and if State could add a couple of additional TDs in the second half, that should be enough. Why run up the score needlessly?

Coach Elmer Layden did some serious thinking between halves. His backfield wasn't that bad. But the line couldn't contain those Ohio State monsters, on offense or defense. Layden reasoned that his second string line couldn't do any worse and, besides, they might just be eager enough for first string jobs to make an impressive showing. It was a gamble, but what could he lose? The game was getting beyond reach. It was only the great punting by Andy Pilney and Bill Shakespeare that kept the score respectable. The Irish punters kept State pinned deep in their own territory. To score, Ohio always had to march a long way.

The change in forward walls seemed to work. Most of the third quarter was spent in Ohio's half of the field, and this time it was the Buckeyes who couldn't mount an attack. On the last play of the period Andy Pilney grabbed a punt on the Ohio 40 and ran it back to the 12 as the gun sounded.

As the final quarter opened, Pilney passed to Frank

Gaul on Ohio's 1-yard line. Steve Miller, subbing for Fred Carideo, took it across. The conversion failed. Score: Ohio State 13, Notre Dame 6.

Approximately two minutes later Pilney was directing another attack as State's offense went dead. Starting from 54 yards away, two passes ate up 36 yards, and a running series went to the 1-yard line. Then a bad break: Steve Miller was belted hard on the next play and fumbled. Karcher, State's left guard, recovered.

Joe Williams took the Buckeyes out of danger by rambling 23 yards around left end, and when State got moving to their own 43, it looked as if they'd found themselves again. But now Notre Dame put some backbone into its defense and Ohio was forced to punt. The kick set the Irish all the way back to their own 22.

Once more the dogged Irish moved to the attack as Ohio State seemed to run out of gas. The Buckeyes kept trying to outthink the opposition instead of overpowering them. They shuttled back and forth between a seven-man line and an eight-man line and threw a diamond defense in the backfield just for good measure. The Irish were accustomed to playing against a 6-2-2-1 defense.

It was Andy Pilney all the way as he took to the air in order to counter the stacked line. He tossed to quarterback Fromhart for 37 yards; he received a pass from Mike Layden for 9 more; he threw for 14 and then threw again to Layden on the 1. Layden stepped over the goal line. Touchdown!

The home town Ohio State rooters sat nervously on the edges of their seats as Notre Dame lined up to add the extra point that would tie the game. And the kick missed! Ohio still led, 13-12.

Less than two minutes remained as Notre Dame kicked off again. Hoping to prevent a long breakaway runback, the Irish kicked short. Ohio retained possession as the hoped-for fumble by a lineman-receiver didn't materialize.

But the break came just one play later as the scrambling Irish line creamed the ball carrier and he fumbled. Notre Dame recovered.

As the crowd went crazy, Andy Pilney went back to pass again. The State secondary dropped off and covered the receivers, the line spread out to give them a hand. There was nobody for Pilney to throw to. So he took off from his own 49, cutting and dodging tacklers, and was finally knocked out of bounds on the 19-yard line. That sortie cost him dearly. Pilney was carried off the field on a stretcher.

In came Bill Shakespeare. Notre Dame lined up and Shakespeare took the snap, then faded back. This time State didn't know what to do. Cover the receivers? Shakespeare could do a lot of running, and the goal line wasn't that far away. Better to rush him. Nobody, it seemed, was watching Wayne Millner. Nobody, that is, except Bill Shakespeare.

He lofted one to Millner standing in the end zone. The sure-handed end grabbed the ball. Score!

The dazed State team took the kickoff with less than half a minute to play. And when their passer tried to get off a last-gasp, heaven-help-us pass, he was brought down by a host of Irish linemen. The gun went off. It was Notre Dame by 18-13!

In 1969, *Sport Magazine* took a poll among active and retired players, coaches, athletic directors and other knowledgeable football people. They wanted to find out which college game was the greatest ever played. The Ohio State-Notre Dame game of 1935 was the overwhelming choice. According to the article, Pilney himself put the finger on what he considered the turning point in the game. He said:

> In the fourth quarter Wally Fromhart, our quarterback, came to the huddle from the bench and told us Layden said we could create history at Notre Dame. That really hit me, coming from Layden, one of the Four Horsemen. No one will ever know how many games tradition has won for Notre Dame. On the practical side, Layden made some changes in our pass patterns over the middle and I completed seven in a row.

So Layden had borrowed a leaf from his own head coach, Knute Rockne. He had inspired his troops to the greatest heights, and they came through for him, as they had done countless times for Rockne.

But the similarity did not end there. Seven years before, Knute Rockne had mesmerized the Irish into a victory over mighty Army. And in the next game they had been trounced by Carnegie Tech. After the Ohio State fray, Notre Dame took on pathetic Northwestern, which had already lost three of its five games.

Northwestern beat Notre Dame, 14-7!

When the Slinger Didn't Sling

Texas Christian vs. Louisiana State—
January 1, 1936

Ask any sportswriter, ask any football coach, ask any fan who has followed the game of football for a couple of decades; ask them to name the ten greatest passers who played in the National Football League, and there isn't a shred of doubt that the same names will be cited by just about everyone: Y. A. Tittle, Johnny Unitas, Otto Graham, Bobby Layne, Bob Waterfield, Sid Luckman, Norm Van Brocklin, Arnie Herber, Bart Starr— and Slingin' Sammy Baugh. Furthermore, if you really pushed those experts and asked them to name the best *all-around* player in that elite group, there isn't any doubt that the man they'd name would be the thrower from Texas Christian University, Sammy Baugh.

Baugh was not only a rifle-armed passer, he was also a fine kicker, ball carrier, and defensive player. He did all those things in college, and he did the same things in professional football, too!

Most of the above-mentioned passers seemed to be born with the natural ability to throw a football, or else they started throwing the pigskin at a very early age. For example, Tittle was already an accomplished passer by the time he entered college. Luckman was given a football by his father and he was the only kid on his Brooklyn block who owned such a treasure, so naturally he was the one who threw it most often.

But for Baugh, neither passing nor football as a whole came easy. In fact he considered himself a baseball player primarily, and his scholarship to T.C.U. was for baseball, not football. He was considered good enough to be signed into the St. Louis Cardinals' farm system as a shortstop. But Baugh was also a realist. He knew his own limitations. The Cards had a shortstop named Marty "Slats" Marion, easily the best in the National League during his playing days. There wasn't any doubt in Baugh's mind that Marty Marion could play the position better even without a glove or spiked shoes. Since Baugh couldn't bear to be second-best at anything, he just quit baseball and went into pro football—and he became first-best.

However, that was later. Sammy Baugh had worked hard to learn how to pass so that he could make his local high school team in Sweetwater, Texas. The position he chose was quarterback, and he also wanted to be the team's passer. Baugh's arm was strong enough, but he often threw high, or low, or wide. That was because shortstops didn't necessarily have to be right on target with a long throw to first base. The man guarding the bag could stretch, or leap, or scoop up the ball on the short hop. But throwing a football was different.

So Baugh began to practice with an old automobile tire suspended from a tree limb by a rope. He threw from all sorts of positions and from long or short distances until he could put the football through the tire almost every time.

Then he set the tire swinging, from side to side, and then forward and backward. He kept practicing until he could thread the needle. He had little trouble making the high school team.

Like any poor kid in a farming area, Sammy Baugh knew that the only way to get somewhere in life was through a college education. He applied to Texas Christian for a baseball scholarship. Freshman football and baseball coach "Dutch" Meyer was there to help him. In filling out his recommendation, Meyer added the words, "He can play a little football, too."

But Sam didn't play much as a freshman, and not a lot as a sophomore either. Sure, he could pass pretty well, but he seemed unsure of himself in college competition. Baugh realized that he had to add something to his passing ability. He didn't have the power or the speed to be a regular ball carrier, but his legs were pretty strong. He could kick pretty well.

"Pretty well" wasn't good enough; so he practiced punting as he had passing. Every minute of his spare time was spent booting a football, and after a while he could boom them out fifty-five and sixty yards on the fly.

As a junior, Baugh came into his own. T.C.U. carved up the Southwest Conference opposition, and in the next-to-last game of the season met Southern Methodist for the championship. It was a bruising game from start to finish.

Both teams scored touchdowns, and both teams fought off additional scores. It was a 14-all game until the big break came for S.M.U. They had marched to the Texas Christian 35 where the drive bogged down. On fourth down and long yardage, Bob Finley dropped back into punt formation, and the T.C.U. secondary relaxed. So Finley faked a kick and threw a pass to Bobby Wilson, who had slipped behind the Texas Christian safety man. Wilson made a leaping catch on the 7-yard line and went in for the touchdown.

Baugh tried to start a Texas drive, and he succeeded in taking the team to the S.M.U. 28. But a fumble took them back to the 35, and a fourth-down play couldn't make back enough yardage for the first down. Texas lost, 20-14.

That game produced two post-season bowl entries. Southern Methodist went to the Rose Bowl, and Texas Christian was invited to play Louisiana State University in the second annual Sugar Bowl classic.

Coach Bernie Moore's L.S.U. Tigers were loaded with outstanding front line players and were deep in good reserves. They had been caught in a 10-7 upset by a strong Rice Institute team, but the Tigers quickly righted themselves and swept the next nine games to become champions of the Southeast Conference. In Abe Mickal, L.S.U. had the best punter in the conference, and Bill Crass was certainly one of the better running backs in the southern tier of states. Gaynell Tinsley at end was strictly all-American, on offense and defense; and the other receiver, Jeff Barrett, had been mentioned once or twice for All-Conference honors. With that kind of attack, L.S.U. figured to win, but not by much.

Dutch Meyer readily admitted that his chances of victory rested on the good right arm of Sammy Baugh. Throughout the Horned Frogs' 11 won, 1 lost season, it was always Slingin' Sammy who delivered when the chips were down. Halfback Jimmy Lawrence took care of much of the running, and Will Walls at end was Sammy's favorite throwing target. Overall, T.C.U. was a good, solid club—when they were all healthy. But Meyer was going into the game with eleven of his twenty-seven-man squad hurting in one way or another. Not many subs were available for action.

Thus Meyer's strategy was obvious: Let Baugh throw as often as possible; try to jump out in front and hold L.S.U. from scoring too often; in short, "hit 'em and hold 'em."

It had rained the day before the game, and Dutch Meyer was worried. Neither Baugh nor anyone else in the world could keep passing consistently with a wet football. Meyer almost wept openly on January 1, because the rain continued and the field was just a 100-yard mess of puddles and goo. Yet there were 35,000 hardy souls in the stands, braving the steady downpour to watch twenty-two men take a communal mudbath.

A sustained Texas passing attack was now out of the question. In the S.M.U. game, Baugh had kept the pressure on, constantly threatening to unload one of his long ones. Now the T.C.U. big gun was spiked before it could fire off a shot. Dutch Meyer set the game plan in the dressing room: a lot of punting, a lot of running, and a lot of praying for the breaks.

The breaks started coming in the second period, but they went against Texas Christian. Darrell Lester, the Horned Frogs' starting center, was added to the injury list. Then the Tigers put on a sustained drive that took them right up to the T.C.U. front door. The Frogs burrowed into the mud and braced themselves.

Four times the hard-hitting L.S.U. backfield cracked into the line, and four times the ball carrier was stacked up. When the series was ended, the ball was on the Texas 2-yard line, but the Frogs had held.

Baugh figured that the smart thing to do was kick out of danger. And he knew L.S.U. figured the same thing. This might be a golden opportunity to catch the Tigers off guard. And a pass might give them a sweet gain.

Texas lined up in short punt formation, with Baugh standing at the edge of his own end zone. He took the snap from center and then drew back his arm to let fly with the pass.

Probably Gaynell Tinsley had visions of blocking the kick to give L.S.U. a 2-point safety, for he fired in there with the snap of the ball. His heart leaped with gladness as he saw Baugh trying to pass, and he chased the Slinger all over the end zone. Baugh slipped and slid and finally the ball squirted out of his hand across the back line of the end zone for an automatic safety.

Those two points on the scoreboard looked like two thousand as the teams returned to action. Within a couple of minutes the Frogs were back in the ball game. For, on the first play from scrimmage after Louisiana State had the ball, Bill Crass fumbled and Will Walls recovered for Texas, back on the Tigers' 40-yard line.

Once more Baugh decided to gamble. The previous pass attempt had ended in disaster. Maybe L.S.U. figured Baugh wouldn't try any more foolish stunts. Baugh still thought a pass might work—provided he didn't throw it. So he fed the ball to Jimmy Lawrence, and Lawrence threw to Will Walls, and the Horned Frogs were on the L.S.U. 17-yard line!

Three Texas running plays got absolutely nowhere. On fourth down Baugh knelt in the mud and spotted the ball, while Talden "Tilly" Manton put it through the uprights from the 26-yard line. Score: 3-2, Texas Christian ahead. The half ended that way.

The rain continued to fall, and the Sugar Bowl field began to look more like a swimming pool than a gridiron. Neither team could mount a sustained attack as the players fell, banged, and skidded into each other. And every time L.S.U. appeared to be sputtering back to life, it was Sammy Baugh who put the brakes to their attack.

Twice in the third quarter he intercepted passes in his own area. And when Texas couldn't move, his booming punts over the L.S.U. goal kept the Tigers pinned in their own territory. Fourteen times that sodden day he put his toe into the football, and he averaged exactly 44.6 yards per punt—which was amazing, considering the condition of the field, his poor footing, and the wet ball. Almost on a par with him was Abe Mickal, who also put on an exhibition of major league punting, averaging 42.2 yards per kick.

The game went into the final quarter, and the fans marveled that those poor souls down on the field could pick themselves up again after a play was over. Neither team let up for an instant. The ball would be snapped, and the lines would collide, and half the players would end up with their faces down in the mud. Ball carriers couldn't cut or change direction, and tacklers would slide past blockers as if they were on water skis. Nobody's number was visible any longer.

Late in the game Sammy Baugh brought the crowd to its feet with a swivel-hipped slosh through the mud for 44 yards, all the way to L.S.U.'s 2-yard line. For a moment it seemed that they'd break the game open there and then. But, as Texas Christian had done before, Louisiana State rose up in all its pent-up fury and smashed down the Texas runners. Four ground plays *lost* 9 yards, and the Tigers took over on downs.

As the game flickered away, L.S.U. tried passes to pull it out, but that failed too when Abe Mickal's last-gasp pass was intercepted by a sub named Harold Mc-Clure. The gun went off with T.C.U. in possession on the L.S.U. 21.

That grueling, bruising L.S.U.-T.C.U. mudbath has come to be known as "the football game with the baseball score." One safety and one field goal were the only markers posted on the scoreboard. Sammy Baugh, considered the best passer in college football, had done next to nothing with his throwing arm. In fact, the Texas passing attack showed three completions out of eleven attempts, good for a meager 53 yards. And all-American receiver Gaynell Tinsley had not exactly covered himself with glory either on offense, although he played a raging defensive game.

Afterward, some people wondered what might have happened on a dry field. And suppose a guy like Baugh had someone like Tinsley on the other end of his passes? Now, wouldn't *that* be a killer combination!

Some people found out. That summer, the College All-Stars played the Green Bay Packers. The college kids won, 6-0. And the TD came on a forward pass from Sammy Baugh to Gaynell Tinsley!

The Champs against the Rookies

College All-Stars vs. Green Bay Packers—
August 3, 1963

In a manner of speaking, it can be said that sportswriters are almost as necessary to athletics as the men and the contests they write about. True, the fame and salaries of sportswriters are not measured by crucial plays missed or successfully executed. They don't run around under a hot sun or in the bitter cold, and not a single one of them is concerned about his batting average, dropped forward passes, or points scored per game. Their value is measured in other ways.

First, naturally, they inform the public. Superstars reach the heights not only because of their heroic deeds on the diamond, the gridiron, the basketball court, et cetera, but also because there are men who record those exploits for posterity in newspapers, magazines, and books. It is the sportswriters who change the perfect athletic robot into a flesh-and-blood human being with all his hangups and aspirations.

And many of the scribes are not simple journeymen hacks, pecking away at typewriters with two fingers, hoping that a copy editor will find and correct their errors in grammar and punctuation. Indeed, several sportswriters have made valuable contributions to literature: Ring Lardner, Damon Runyon, and Jimmy Cannon are but a few of the widely admired writers who have pounded out words about sports heroes. And Arthur Daley of *The New York Times* won a Pulitzer Prize when he successfully—and humorously—untangled the garbled syntax of Casey Stengel, manager of the New York Yankees.

Arch Ward of the Chicago *Tribune* was one of the most revered members of the sportswriting fraternity. Through the efforts of the man and the newspaper, one of the great traditions in professional athletics was established—the baseball and football All-Star games. After several discussions between Ward and George "Papa Bear" Halas, owner of the Chicago Bears, the format of the football game was worked out. And over the years the greatest beneficiary of these annual classics has been the Chicago Tribune Charities, Inc. After normal expenses are deducted, large sums of money are distributed to United Charities, Catholic Charities, and Jewish Charities in and around the city of Chicago.

On paper, that first All-Star game seemed to be a gross mismatch. In 1933 the Bears had defeated the New York Giants to become the first NFL champions. And although nobody could foresee the future, they were destined to go through the 1934 season undefeated and untied! How could those college kids hope to compete with such all-time greats as Bronco Nagurski, the wild bull from Minnesota, who ate tacklers as a mid-afternoon snack, or "Automatic" Jack Manders, who missed a field goal attempt about once every two years.

However, those college All-Stars were much tougher

than anyone imagined. As 77,450 fans looked on, the rookies and the champs battled to a scoreless deadlock. The following year, Chicago played the college All-Stars again and were lucky enough to edge out a 5-0 victory. The third year, with the Detroit Lions facing the up-and-coming youngsters, the game ended in a 7-7 tie. Then, in 1937 the boys with the new diplomas took a 6-0 decision from Green Bay. The only score of the contest came when one of the greatest of all passers, Slingin' Sammy Baugh, flipped a scoring strike to one of the greatest of all receivers, Gaynell Tinsley.

The 1938 game ended in a fantastic upset. Sparked by another passing immortal, Cecil Isbell of Purdue, the All-Stars racked up the Washington Redskins, 28-16. Isbell passed for one touchdown, a 39-yard beauty to John Kovatch of Northwestern, and Indiana's Corby Davis bucked over for another TD from the 1-foot line. The other two touchdowns were the results of pass interceptions. Phil Dougherty of Santa Clara and Andy Uram of Minnesota each counted with a 40-yard run after picking off errant passes.

It wasn't long, however, before the professionals asserted their superiority over the fledglings. Not that the pros were so much better, man for man; in fact, the All-Star lineups were choked with high draft choices, and many of them went on to become great players. The pros had a few things going for them which the college kids couldn't always overcome.

First, the All-Stars were playing a *team*. Each veteran had at least one year of experience in pro football and had played with the club through a whole season. A defensive tackle knew how the defensive end alongside him moved, how he shifted, how he blocked out his opponent. The

College All-Stars had never played together as a unit and had only a few short weeks to prepare an attack and a defense. Teams need time to "jell."

Second was a psychological hangup. The kids were playing the champions of pro football. Their opponents had beaten the other professional teams consistently. Sure, the kids were cocky and eager to pit themselves against the champs. But deep down they knew how good the pros were. And that counted too.

So, year after year, the best of the college players were thrown in with the best team in pro football. The rookies usually gave a good account of themselves, but they lost more than twice as often as they won. The pros would take them apart scientifically, methodically, and these All-Stars had to take the roughing-up with good grace. What else could they do?

The 1962 game was a case in point. The College All-Stars put together a team which, by any standards, was loaded with future talent. There were two dandy passers in Roman Gabriel and Johnny Hadl; two standout receivers in Lance Alworth and Gary Collins; a batch of marvelous running backs, including Ron Bull and Ernie Davis (the latter a tragic victim of leukemia; he never did get to play a regular season of pro football); and Merlin Olsen, one of the best defensive linemen ever to come into football.

So what happened? The Green Bay Packers chopped them into tiny pieces and had hardly any difficulty at all in winning by a score of 42-20.

The 1963 game seemed destined to produce the same result. Once more those rugged Packers were pro football champions. And again the College All-Stars fielded a team which—today—could be the makings of an All-Star all-pro club.

The diploma kids went to Chicago with four of the nation's best quarterbacks: Heisman Trophy winner Terry Baker, Jake "Sonny" Gibbs, Ron VanderKelen, and Glynn Griffing. The running backs included Bill "Thunder" Thornton, Ben Wilson, Charlie Mitchell, and Larry Ferguson, all of whom had received plenty of publicity during their college careers. Catching the passes were the likes of Paul Flately, Pat Richter, and John Mackey. And that defense! Consider these stalwarts and think about their past deeds in pro football: Junius "Buck" Buchanan, Bobby Bell, Lee Roy Jordan, Dave Robinson, Jim Kanicki, Lee Roy Caffee.

Yet the "experts" gave them absolutely no chance at all. In fact, *The New York Times* solemnly stated that the odds against an All-Star victory were about 50-to-1 and that if the Packers won by only two touchdowns, the kids could walk off the field feeling they had won a moral victory.

The team they called the "Pack" was clearly in a class by itself. For two consecutives years it had ruled pro football with an iron hand. Goaded to the heights by head coach Vince Lombardi, Green Bay was a kind of throwback to the days when football was considered such a savage game that President Theodore Roosevelt himself demanded that the rules be changed so that it would become a "safer" sport.

It was said of the Pack that no club could run against it. That line and those linebackers were just too tough. Passes weren't too successful either because of the presence of Herb Adderly, Willie Wood, and Jess Whittenton in the deep secondary.

The offense was one of the most efficient machines ever devised to play the game of football. Bart Starr was the passing robot who pumped the ball into the hands of all-pro receivers Max McGee, Boyd Dowler, and Ron Kramer. Jim Taylor was the second best fullback in the world, with only Cleveland's Jimmy Brown ahead of him. But All-Star coach Otto Graham wasn't overly impressed. For he saw three weaknesses in the Green Bay team, soft spots which had not been there the previous year.

First, defensive end Bill Quinlan was gone. Flamboyant, trigger-tempered, always ready to pick a fight with a teammate or member of the opposition club, Quinlan was a very tough boy indeed. But his carefree ways had soured Lombardi on the big lineman. His place was taken by veteran Urban Henry, a 270-pound monster. But Henry wasn't as fast or as sure as Quinlan.

Second, Ray Nitschke was out of the lineup with injuries. Nitschke was the core of the Green Bay trio of linebackers, the guy who always came up with the big defensive play when it was needed most. Young Ken Iman took his place.

Third, Paul "Golden Boy" Hornung was sitting out the entire season because of a betting scandal. Actually, Hornung had never thrown a game or shaved points or done anything to hurt the team in any way. But he had associated with gamblers, and he had placed bets on games; that was wrong and he knew it. Commissioner Pete Rozelle banished him from football for the 1963 season. His substitute was Tom Moore, a very good running back indeed, but not quite up to Hornung standards.

Before the game was five minutes old, it seemed that the 50-to-1 odds were too short, and that Green Bay would run these wet-behind-the-ears kids right out of Soldier's Field. The Pack took the kickoff, probed around a bit, and was forced to punt. Boyd Dowler got off a 57-yard beauty that was downed on the All-Star 8-yard line.

The Stars tried two plays and didn't get very far. On third down halfback Larry Ferguson fumbled, and the alert Willie Davis recovered on the 11-yard line. Three plays later, Jim Taylor bulled his way in from the 2-yard line. Jerry Kramer added the conversion, and the Packers led, 7-0.

Perhaps the experts were smug about the quick score, but the Stars weren't by any means overwhelmed. Perhaps the man who was least impressed was young Ron Vander-Kelen, who started the game at quarterback. Only a few months before, when it seemed that they were hopelessly out of it, the passer with the scrambling style of play and the unquenchable spirit had almost pulled the Rose Bowl game out of the fire for Wisconsin. All right, the Pack was ahead by a touchdown—so what? There were fifty-five minutes left to play, and that was plenty of time.

The All-Stars, under VanderKelen's leadership, began to roll. Ferguson atoned for his fumble by sliding around end for 11 yards. Vandy fired the ball on the button, hitting Flatley for 15 yards, and then hitting right end Bob Jencks for 9 yards and again for 6 yards. The Stars kept pushing Green Bay back across the chalk marks until they arrived at the Packer 14. There the drive bogged down. Jencks booted the ball through the uprights from the 20. Score now: 7-3, Green Bay leading.

This was not to be one of Bart Starr's better nights. Usually, Starr was an expert at picking up the needed yardage on third-down plays. He sent halfback Tom Moore to the sidelines on a pass pattern, and his throw seemed to be on target—almost. At the last second, 6-foot, 4-inch defensive Tommy Janik stepped in front of Moore, plucked the ball out of the air, and took off. He twisted and turned and dodged for 29 yards, reaching the Green Bay 27 before he was dropped.

Once more VanderKelen went to work. The first play fizzled, but on the next one Pat Richter went into a crowd of three Green Bay defenders and grabbed Vandy's flip, good for 21 yards to the Packer 6-yard line.

On the first play of the second quarter, Larry Ferguson wiped out the memory of his fumble completely as he followed wipe-out blocking by Bob Vogel and Ed Budde all the way into the end zone. The kick made it 10-7, All-Stars.

Back came Green Bay with a drive of its own, and less than five minutes later the score was tied as Jerry Kramer's field-goal attempt from the 21 sailed through the uprights.

That ended the scoring for the half, although the All-Stars almost untied the game. They had gone deep into Packer territory, and in the final seconds tried a field goal from the 19. But Herb Adderley broke through and blocked it.

VanderKelen had played the entire first half, and as the second half opened, Otto Graham played eeny-meeny-miney-mo to see which of his three remaining passers would take over. He settled on Glynn Griffing, the all-American from Mississippi; Griffing was slated to go to the New York Giants after the ball game, and probably Graham wanted Giant coach Allie Sherman to see what his rookie prospect could do.

Griffing did all right—for a while. The All-Stars chalked up two first downs and seemed to be on the move. But then his pass flew into the wrong arms as Herb Adderley got there first and returned the ball to the Stars' 20. However, no great damage was done. Two plays gained 4 yards, and when Jim Taylor lowered his head to smash into the line on third down, he was met by the outstretched arms of Bobby Bell, Lee Roy Jordan, and Don Brumm, who stacked him up for no gain. Surprisingly, Jerry Kramer's try for the 3-pointer from close in went awry.

Time after time Green Bay threatened to open up, starting up good marches and moving steadily, but something always happened to stop this team of champions. Late in the third period the Pack ground out the yardage and had a first down on the All-Star 13. But once again Jim Taylor failed. He fumbled and Don Brabham recovered for the college boys.

Then came one of the most stunning sequences in the entire game. The Stars were growing more confident by the minute, and they decided that perhaps it was possible to run against the Packer line. That's just what they did!

Charlie Mitchell began the series of plays by going around left end for 5 yards. Thunder Thornton, the big fulback from Nebraska, and Mitchell took turns piling into the Green Bay defense. After Mitchell's 5-yard run, he plugged ahead for 3 more, then 7 additional yards. Thornton bucked for 5, then he ricocheted off a tackler and went for 16 yards before he was dumped. Mitchell busted through tackle and rammed ahead for 18. Ben Wilson replaced Thornton and joined in the fun with a 7-yard ramble.

Would the running attack have made it all the way to pay dirt had it been allowed to continue? Who can tell? Certainly the Packers seemed to be upset. How was it possible for these upstarts to stay on the ground with a ball-control game and rack up 61 yards? Why, that was a

Green Bay specialty. Other teams in the NFL had tried to run against the Packers without success, yet the rookies were really rolling up the first downs.

Suddenly Griffing decided to switch tactics. Wilson's run had set up a second-and-3 situation for the All-Stars around the 27-yard line. The Mississippi quarterback went upstairs, but the pass missed connections. Another pass gained exactly 1 yard. Faced with a fourth down and still 2 yards to go, the Stars wisely decided to go for the field goal. Jencks made it good with a 33-yard boot. Score: All-Stars 13, Green Bay 10. And now the sixty-five thousand fans in attendance seemed to sense a staggering upset in the making.

Green Bay was far from finished. No football team composed of human beings could push them around and get away with it for long. Elijah Pitts got his hands on the ball and broke through the college defenses. Only safety man Kermit Alexander stood between Pitts and pay dirt. And Alexander got him! He nailed Pitts after a 43-yard scamper.

The lead touchdown was just a few chalk stripes away. With the ball on the All-Star 17, Pitts got the call again. But left end Fred Miller and right end Don Brumm tore across the line of scrimmage and converged on the luckless Pitts, belting him down for an 8-yard loss. Starr tried to cross up the hard-charging line on the next play, and his choice of plays was a smart one: a screen to Jim Taylor out in the left flat. Sure enough, as the Packer passer dropped all the way back, the line went after him, running right by Taylor. Starr stopped and flipped the ball to his fullback.

The trouble was that Bobby Bell, Minnesota's all-

American linebacker, wasn't fooled at all. He smelled out the play as soon as he saw Starr backpedal more than normal distance. He looked around and saw Taylor near the sideline. Before the Packer back could get his powerful legs pistoning, Bell was in on him and smacked him down for a 6-yard loss.

Driven back to the 31, Green Bay decided to go for the tie with a field goal. And once more Jerry Kramer blew a scoring opportunity, for his 37-yard try missed the mark.

The Stars took over on their own 20, with Ron VanderKelen running the team again. Thunder Thornton got a pair of yards with a line plunge, and Charlie Mitchell picked up 4 more. It was third down, 4 to go. In the huddle, VanderKelen was told that coach Graham wanted him to try a pass to Pat Richter along the sideline. Not a heaven-help-us, go-for-broke throw, but a short one, just enough to pick up the first down.

Vandy took the snap from center and rolled out of his left. Sure enough there was Richter in perfect position to take the pass, and he got it. The first down was in the bag—only Richter didn't stop there. He turned to move up the sideline, and Jess Whittenton got a crack at him. Somehow, Richter shook off the tackle and kept going. And suddenly he was out in the clear with a wall of All-Star blockers surrounding him, convoying the left end through the perils of the Green Bay secondary. From start to finish the play covered almost 74 yards, and the Stars had a 20-10 lead!

Slightly more than three minutes remained when the Pack got the ball again. Starr drove and passed and shoved the team down the field, and with 6 seconds left on the clock Jim Taylor bucked over from the 1-yard line for his second touchdown of the game. But who cared? The mighty Green Bay Packers had fallen before the fired-up rookies! Final score: All-Stars 20, Green Bay Packers 17.

How did it happen? What was the secert of the All-Star success? Well, in part it was the astute decisions made by coach Otto Graham. He thought that the absence of Bill Quinlan would hurt the Packers some, and it did. Urban Henry, the new face in the lineup, was new with the Pack (although he was a seasoned player). And the absence of all-pro linebacker Ray Nitschke didn't help the Green Bay cause. Tom Moore did all right, but Paul Hornung was sorely missed.

And then there were the imponderables which nobody could figure out in advance. Would any gambler have bet that Jim Taylor would be held to a mere 51 yards gained in sixteen carries—slightly more than 3 yards per carry? How about Jerry Kramer missing two easy field goals, a total of 6 points, which would have made the difference? And several times the usually reliable Packer receivers had committed the unforgivable sin of dropping the ball when it was right in their hands.

So the 1963 All-Star team disbanded and returned to the various pro teams which had signed them. It's interesting, looking back across the years, to see which ones made it as professional football players and which ones fell by the wayside.

Oddly, none of the four star passers became front-ranking pro quarterbacks. In fact Jack Gibbs, who didn't get into the game, became a baseball player, joining the New York Yankees as a catcher. Glynn Griffing failed to stick with the New York Giants and eventually dropped out of football. The hero of the game, Ron VanderKelen, failed to reach the heights with Minnesota's Vikings. (An added oddity is that Vandy was a native of Green Bay!)

There were plenty of others on the team who became authentic pro football stars, including Bobby Bell, Pat Richter, Paul Flatley, Buck Buchanan, and John Mackey, to name only a handful.

But, whether they hit or missed, for one night that bunch of kids dominated the football scene. It was Thunder Thornton who said it best. As the All-Stars danced around the locker room, flushed with victory, Thornton let out a tremendous whoop and shouted, "How about that! We killed a dragon!"

Almost Doesn't Count

Army vs. Navy—
December 1, 1946; December 7, 1963

Traditions 'don't just happen, nor are they born full-grown. Most traditions begin life as remembered events, and if the events hold special interest or meaning, they are repeated. For example, it is an American tradition to feast on Thanksgiving Day in honor of the feast of thanksgiving held by the Pilgrims and the Indians back in the seventeenth century. The eating of *matzoh*, or unleavened bread, is one of the Hebrew traditions celebrating Passover and the great exodus from Egypt. It's also traditional for the President of the United States to throw out the first ball for the opening of the baseball season.

Back in 1890 the midshipmen at Annapolis had a pretty good football team. West Point didn't have any football team at all. But there was already a rivalry building between these two fine institutions, and when Navy issued a football challenge, Army had to accept. An Army cadet named Dennis Michie, one of the few at West Point who had tried his hand at the game, rounded up some of the best athletes at the Point and gave them some quick instruction.

When the Navy boys arrived at the meadow near the Point, they noticed a beat-up old goat wandering around aimlessly. The poor beast was promptly commandeered. Thus both traditions, that of an Army-Navy football game and the use of a goat as Navy's official mascot, can be traced back to November 29, 1890.

The Army team tried hard but was no match for the more experienced sailors, and Navy won, 24-0. Since no self-respecting bunch of athletes takes a licking the first time out without demanding a rematch, Army wanted another chance. Navy obliged. The next year "Brave Old Army Team" went to Annapolis and put the slug on the midshipmen, 32-16.

That, in brief, is how the Army-Navy football tradition began. Later, a football stadium was built at West Point and named Michie Field, in honor of the cadet who first taught his classmates the rudiments of the game. (Michie, incidentally, was killed leading a charge up San Juan Hill in the Spanish-American War.)

There is one thing about any traditional game that never changes, no matter which teams are involved: regardless of how bad a season has been, it's considered a success when one traditional rival beats the other. Past records don't mean a thing under such circumstances; even the lowliest underdog can rise to the heights and pull off an upset. Back in 1948, for instance, Army was undefeated and Navy hadn't won a game all season when the two teams butted heads. Navy rallied and tied Army, 21-all, and the men in blue went back to Annapolis in a splendid frame of mind.

It is by no means unusual for one of the service

academies to come up with a team of championship caliber. In 1954, Navy's "Team Named Desire" won the Eastern title and beat a pretty good Army squad, 27-20, in the final game of the year for both clubs. Each team has come up with some magnificent players: Slade Cutter, Joe Bellino, and Roger Staubach have shone for the Middie teams, and such stalwarts as Elmer Oliphant, Pete Dawkins, and Bob Anderson have stood out as greats for Army. But there is no argument as to which was the greatest of the service academy football combinations: the superb Army team of 1944-46. This was a team which might have beaten a number of pro outfits of that era.

In the line were a great group of sixty-minute players, including the likes of Goble Bryant, Hank Foldberg, Joe Steffy, Barney Poole, and John Trent. Rip Rowan backed up the line on defense and played right halfback on offense. Arnold Tucker was one of the gamest, greatest quarterbacks ever to come to the Point.

But it was the one-two punch of Glenn Davis—"Mr. Outside"—and Doc Blanchard—"Mr. Inside"—that struck terror into the hearts of the opposition. They were the basic reason for Army's ranking as the number-one college team in the nation. They really put the word "all" into the phrase "all-American."

Were a couple of yards needed for a first down? Feed it to Doc Blanchard and get out of his way. The heavy-legged Army fullback would pile into the line and then give it that second effort to put the ball where it was supposed to go. He was a murderous blocker, a sure-handed receiver, a bulldozing runner.

And how good was Mr. Outside, Glenn Davis? Good enough to turn pro and win a steady job with the Los

Angeles Rams later on. In his Army football career, Davis scored *71 touchdowns!* He could also throw the football as well as most starting quarterbacks. In 1946 Davis completed 17 of 45 attempts for 12 touchdowns!

That explosive backfield trio—Blanchard, Davis, and Tucker—spent three years together on the varsity, starting in 1944. The 1946 Navy game was their last as a unit. In fact the whole Army team was to be broken up by graduation. And perhaps that was just as well, for the team was starting to fray at the seams.

The starters were as good as ever but beset by injuries. The regulars were taking a severe pounding, and they had to hang in there because the reserves weren't as good as before. That explained the 0-0 tie with Notre Dame during the 1946 season. It had been a rough year, but Army came up to the Navy game unbeaten. Its string of 27 games without a defeat was still intact.

Navy, on the other hand, was suffering through one of its worst seasons ever. They had beaten Villanova in the opener, then dropped the next seven in a row. True, they weren't *that* bad; some of the defeats had been last-minute heartbreakers. Still, nobody rolled over and played dead at the sight of them, the way some teams did when Army showed up. The 1946 Navy team was a 28 point underdog at game time.

Had anyone bothered to analyze the game in detail, it would have been apparent immediately that the 4-touchdown spread was ridiculous. In spite if its solid defense, Army's scoring power lay with Tucker, Blanchard, and Davis, and two-thirds of that offense was hurting bad.

Doc Blanchard had torn ligaments in his knees. Arnold Tucker, racked up in the Penn game, also had an injured knee and a slight shoulder separation. Only Davis was healthy, but he couldn't be expected to go it alone. When he tried, the opposition zeroed in on him and belted Mr. Outside with jolly abandon. Davis had been the mainstay in the Oklahoma game, when Blanchard was hobbling around, and the Sooners had made merry with their tackles, bringing down the halfback with a mighty thud every time he carried the ball. But he had taken Army through to victory.

At the outset, Navy tried to throw the Army line off its timing by alternating between the standard T formation and a single wing with unbalanced line. It worked pretty well for a while until the Army defense got the hang of what Navy was up to, at which point they held on their own 45. The teams then traded fumble recoveries. At last Army found themselves in possession on their own 37, and was able to start moving.

The big blow was a Tucker-to-Davis pass that carried all the way to Navy's 14. Blanchard went up the middle for a yard to tighten up the defense still more, and then Tucker fed it to Davis again; the little scatback buzzed through the befuddled Middies for the touchdown. The extra point made it 7-0, Army.

The touchdown seemed to light a fire under Navy, for they bounced back very quickly and started a long march of their own. From their own 19, they kept banging away in short power plays and quick passes. Running backs Pete Williams and Myron Gerber kept the Army line and secondary honest with bucks into the center, while passer Reaves Baysinger threw to his ends, Leon Bramlett and Art Markel. On the second play of the second period, Baysinger went over on a keeper play.

The conversion was missed. Army still had a 1-point edge.

Now it was time for the West Pointers to show how good they could be. Though Blanchard was limping a bit, he and Davis kept grinding it out until they reached the Army 47. Navy seemed to sense a ground smash by Blanchard and bunched into a seven-man line. That left the secondary to cover a lot of open territory. The next play was a Blanchard run, all right, and it worked out against Navy. Mr. Inside picked up a key block on the trap play, cut over to the sidelines, and he was gone! The kick made it 14-6, Army.

Shortly before the half ended, Army picked off a Navy pass and started out again toward the Navy goal. On the Middie 26, Tucker called for a pass. Only he wasn't going to throw it; Davis was elected to do the honors.

Blanchard and Rowan exchanged places in the formation, with Mr. Inside playing wide and Rowan in the fullback slot. Davis dropped back while Blanchard ran a stop-and-go buttonhook pattern around the defensive halfback. Davis faked a pass in one direction and then threw to Blanchard who was wide open. The big fullback scored his second TD of the day. Halftime saw the score at 21-6.

Strangely, Navy was more convinced than ever that they would win the game. There was something missing from the Army attack, a spark of confidence, a sureness of victory. It was almost as if Blanchard, Davis, and company were simply trying to hold on, wait for the breaks, and eke out the win in this final game of their college careers.

Navy's instinct was sound, and it became evident

early in the third period that Army was playing on nerve alone. A West Point march bogged down near the Navy 31; Army was faced with a fourth-and-2 situation.

Normally, there would have been no question as to Army's next play: go for it. With a two-touchdown lead, what could they lose? There was always the possibility that a Blanchard smash or a Davis sweep or a pass from either Tucker or Davis could make a mere 2 yards. But this wasn't a usual situation. Tucker's leg hurt so much he could barely stand erect. Blanchard's knee was in bad shape, and he limped to and from the huddle.

Tucker elected to punt. Davis kicked for the coffin corner but he didn't do too well, and Navy took over near its own 20.

Now the gutsy Army quarterback had to come out of the game, at least on defense. Anyone else would have been in the infirmary; but this game guy stayed on the sidelines, ready to come back into the lineup when and if Army got its hands on the football again.

Navy began to grind it out, shoving the Army line back, back, back, and then they were on the West Point 18, with a fourth down staring at them. Bill Hawkins of Navy (playing with a bad leg, too, but these men of West Point and Annapolis never quit when they faced each other until they were unconscious!) pulled off the buck-lateral to perfection. He took two steps toward the line, stopped, and fired a lateral pass to Pete Williams, who carried all the way to Army's 3-yard line. From there Hawkins rode it across. Once again the conversion was missed. Score: 21-12, Army.

The four-touchdown pre-game victory prediction now seemed completely foolish. Army was in trouble and everybody in the stands knew it. The West Pointers

Drawing of the first college football game played between Rutgers and Princeton in November, 1869. Rutgers won six goals to four.

This is the Army vs Notre Dame game in November, 1928, when coach Knute Rockne said, "Win this one for the Gipper."

Albie Booth of Yale (in white helmet) carrying the ball for a small gain against Dartmouth, October, 1931.

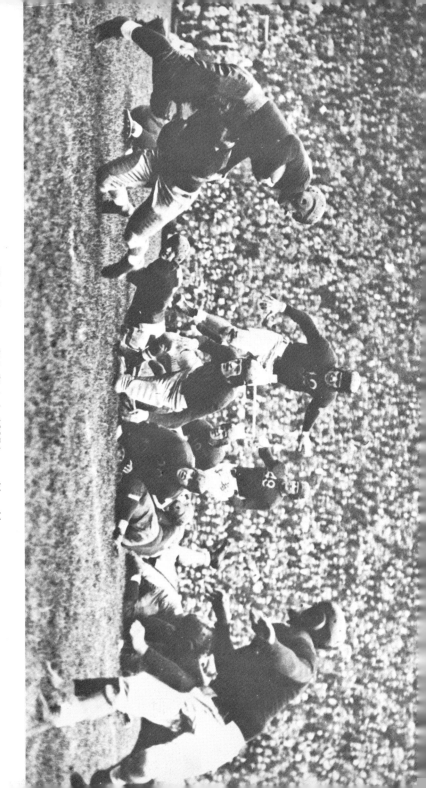

Notre Dame vs Ohio State in 1935 is considered by many as the greatest college game ever played.

In 1963 the All Stars killed the dragon by beating The Green Bay Packers, 20-17. Vanderkelen of Wisconsin dives for short gain.

Army's Felix Blanchard (35) on a 64-yard touchdown run against Navy at Philadelphia, in November, 1946.

Navy's Roger Staubach makes his way downfield as the Navy won against Army, 21-15, when they played in December, 1963.

Texas' Ernie Koy (23) helps beat Joe Namath and Alabama by scampering 79 yards for a touchdown as Texas won at the 1965 Orange Bowl, 14-7.

Paul Hornung (5) of the Green Bay Packers dives over the goal line in the 1965 play-off game against the Baltimore Colts.

Packers fullback Jim Taylor (31) on a twenty-yard run
against Baltimore, in December, 1966. Score 14-10.

In the 1967 NFL title game Packers linebacker Robinson drapes over QB Meredith of Dallas. The pass was intercepted.

The Jets' Joe Namath creamed by Raiders' Carleton Oats
(85) in play-off game at Shea Stadium in November, 1968.

The Harvard-Yale classic ended in a tie in 1968. Both teams had won the Ivy League title that year. Both had undefeated seasons.

Donny Anderson (44) steps over the goal line for the Packers' fourth touchdown in the Super Bowl, 1968.

Namath hands off to Emerson Boozer (32) as Jets' won the Super Bowl against the Colts in 1969.

Len Dawson of the Kansas City Chiefs gets off a pass that helped defeat the Vikings in the Super Bowl Game of 1970.

brought the kickoff back to the 25, and then Davis and Blanchard tried to move the ball, but it was tough going. Between them they carried just over nine yards in a trio of running plays. It was fourth down, about two feet to go, maybe even less.

They were dangerously close to their own goal, but Tucker sought to bring the team back up again. He called on the limping Blanchard to go for it. Mr. Inside banged into the middle of the Navy line and bounced back. Navy took over on downs!

Navy sprang to the attack. Two quick plays—a 14-yard pass to Bramlett and a slice through the center by Hawkins—put the ball on Army's 5-yard line. Hawkins bulled for 2 yards more to open the final quarter. Then a lateral-forward put it over; Baysinger lobbed the ball to reserve halfback Bill Earl, who tossed the forward pass to Leon Bramlett in the corner. Bill Gustafson, replacing Arnold Tucker, was bewildered by all the throwing in the backfield and couldn't stop the touchdown pass. Once more the conversion was missed, but the score was now 21-18, with most of the final quarter still left.

Neither team could put it all together for the next six minutes, but with half the period to play, Navy took possession on its own 33 and began a last-ditch march to pull out the ball game. Onward they marched to the Army 23; and on a fourth-down play sub running back Lynn Chewning clawed his way through for 20 yards, all the way to the 3. First and goal with ninety seconds to play!

The shrieking crowd spilled out of the stands and converged on the sidelines. Some of the spectators were actually standing a foot or two inside the playing area itself, but it was impossible for the ushers to get rid of them all. Besides, everybody was watching the action on the field, where a stunning upset was in the making.

On first down Chewning tore into the line, but Goble Bryant and Hank Foldberg stopped him cold. Chewning went up the middle again, and this time Barney Poole grabbed him.

Then came one of those thoughtless mistakes that can foul up even the steadiest plans. Bill Hawkins came in to replace Chewning, but it took so long for him to tell his teammates the new play to be used that the referee slapped on a 5-yard penalty for delay of the game. Navy went back to the Army 8-yard line.

The play to be run was that buck-lateral which had worked so well for Navy's second touchdown. Only this time it didn't work. Barney Poole saw what was coming, and he chased the receiver to the sidelines; that is, the play went where the sidelines should have been, except that it was hidden by spectators. The ball was spotted on Army's 4-yard line.

Now came the foul-up. The clock was still running. Probably the officials didn't think the receiver had run out of bounds. But he couldn't get to the sidelines because of the crowd, so wasn't that the same thing as going out of bounds? Evidently not, because the sweepsecond hand on the clock was still moving.

Bill Earl came racing in to report into the game, ask for a time out, do anything at all to stop the clock. He was too late! The gun went off. It was all over, and Army had won, 21-18, preserving its undefeated record. For Navy it was a moral victory.

That single game has always been considered the greatest of all Army-Navy contests. Maybe it was. But there was another one on December 7, 1963, which was almost as magnificent. And it was remarkable how history repeated itself—only in reverse!

The tragedy of November 22, 1963, when President John F. Kennedy was gunned down by an assassin, put a damper on all sports for many months. For a time it was rumored that the Army-Navy game would be called off in memory of the fallen President. But then it was decided that to cancel the game would serve no purpose. John Kennedy had always been devoted to all athletic contests, especially football. The games of touch football on the White House lawn were almost legendary. All sorts of prominent figures participated, including the President himself, his brother Robert (the Attorney General) and his brother Edward (Senator from Massachusetts). In a sense the Army-Navy game was almost a memorial to the departed Chief Executive. Naturally enough he had secretly rooted for Navy, but that was understandable, for his wartime record as commander of a PT boat in the Pacific was known to every American. However, he tried to show no partiality. Before the 1961 game, he sent a note to both Army and Navy, which read in part:

"It is easy to pick the real winner of the annual Army-Navy football game: the people of the United States."

Both teams had already won a goodly share of their scheduled games. Army had been beaten only by Minnesota and Pittsburgh; Navy was ranked second in the nation, having lost only to a good Southern Methodist team in a real squeaker.

Spearheading the Navy attack was the all-American

quarterback, Roger Staubach, who had won the Heisman Trophy in his junior year at the Academy. He was the rollout type; Staubach could pass with pinpoint accuracy and also run with the ball like a halfback. In fact, one of Navy's good plays was the quarterback draw. Staubach would drop back, and the offensive line would allow the defense to curve around into the backfield. Meanwhile, potential receivers would head for the sidelines. With the whole center area cleared out, Staubach would fake a throw, tuck the ball under his arm and go straight up the middle. Generally the play gained substantial yardage.

Navy also had a very fine backfield to do the running: the fleet Johnny Sai, one of the fastest halfbacks in the East; Pat Donnelly, a powerhouse fullback; and Bob Teall, a good receiver on the flank.

Underdog Army drew first blood. Taking over on their own 41, the Black Knights went relentlessly across the Navy goal, sparked by their own rollout quarterback, Carl "Rollie" Stichweh. The young man from Long Island finished the march himself, sprinting around end for 10 yards and the touchdown. The conversion was good.

Navy refused to panic, even when things didn't quite work out. Mixing his plays beautifully, Staubach led his flotilla across the striped field. Two passes really stung Army: a 22 yarder to end Neil Henderson and another to Bob Teall for 20 more. But Army held and took the ball away on its own 1-yard line.

So Staubach started all over again, and once more it seemed that Navy would be thwarted in its bid to tie the game. Roger the Dodger rolled out to his left, stopped, and fired a 32-yard pass to his right end, Gary

Kellner. Kellner scored, but the touchdown was nullified as Navy was caught holding. Undaunted, Staubach took the 15-yard penalty and picked up where he had left off. In 6 plays Navy went the distance. The quarterback ran the option for 10, passed to Johnny Sai for 27 and then pulled the quarterback draw specialty for 8 yards. The touchdown came on a 4-yard line plunge by Pat Donnelly. At intermission the score was 7-all.

Navy came out for the second half determined to establish its superiority once and for all. Staubach called a beautiful series, never letting Army get set up. Two passes totaled 27 yards, and a run by Donnelly gained 20. It was a combined air and ground attack at its best. Pat Donnelly went across from the 6-inch line. Navy led, 14-7.

Every once in a while a team must make a decision, and sometimes the whole ball game can turn on what happens next. In Army's case it was a question as to whether or not to accept a penalty call.

The Black Knights had intercepted a Staubach toss and rolled toward Navy's end zone. They had a first down on the Navy 17, and a nice run took it to the 9. But Navy was offside on the play, and the referee gave Army a choice: if the Kaydets took the penalty, the ball would go back to the 12, first down and 5 to go. If they refused, the ball would stay on the 9, giving them a second-down situation with 2 to go. In other words Army would lose 3 yards but gain a very important down.

West Point elected to take the run and refuse the penalty. They figured that 2 yards wasn't much when they had the momentum and three chances to get the first down. However, Navy's line suddenly found back-bone, and on fourth down the ball carrier was dropped for a loss. Navy took over on downs.

Staubach was quick to capitalize on the turnover of the football. In five plays and two penalties Navy had crossed Army's goal again. The clock on the scoreboard showed ten minutes and thirty-two seconds left when the conversion made the score 21-7, Navy ahead.

But the men of Annapolis did not regain possession of the ball for the rest of the game!

A big runback of the kickoff set up Army's next shot at their naval rivals. Stichweh kept pounding the line, refusing to risk an interception. Navy thought that Army had to pass to get back on the scoreboard, and Stichweh crossed them with stabs into the line by his running backs, Ken Waldrop and Ray Paske. It was slow, but steady, and finally the Army quarterback wedged out the score from the 1-yard line.

Stichweh wasn't playing for the tie. He wanted the win. So he ran around end for the 2-point conversion and now Army trailed by 21-15. One more touchdown, plus the conversion, would put the Black Knights into the lead!

Maybe Navy wasn't ready for the on-side kick, or maybe the skittering boot was too well-placed to be recovered. The Army gang went after the free ball, and it was taken by none other than the quarterback himself, Rollie Stichweh. There were six minutes left, and the badly rattled Navy crew were wondering what hit them.

Now Army resumed its pounding of the Navy line. It was Waldrop for 4, Paske for 12, then Waldrop, Paske, and Stichweh all the way to the 23. As Navy's secondary pulled in close, Stichweh crossed them up with a pass to Parcells on the 7!

One minute and thirty-eight seconds remained as Army slammed into the Navy line's center. Paske hit to the 5, Waldrop went to the 4, and one more ground play went to the 2. Fourth down, goal to go. It all boiled down to the last play.

Or did it?

The stadium was a bedlam of noise as the clock kept on ticking away. Nobody could hear anything except screams and yells and the roaring, indistinguishable noises that crowds make when everyone is excited. In desperation Stichweh turned to the officials. He held up his arms pleading for quiet, and tried to ask for a time out. But the referee didn't hear him. He couldn't have heard any individual's voice if his very existence depended on it. No time out was called. The puzzled Kaydets looked around to see what was happening. And the gun went off! The game was over, and Navy had won, 21-15!

Thus did two Army-Navy games end in near upsets in the shadow of the favored team's goalposts. Each time the referee could not help the underdog team because of what the crowd did. Once Army had held on tight and kept the victory because of the mob on the sidelines, and the other time it was Navy benefiting from the noise of the spectators.

And yet, in itself, that repetition of history in reverse wasn't so unusual. There's always something different on tap when a game of football is played between traditional rivals.

One for the Money—
Two for the Show

Alabama vs. Texas—
January 1, 1965;

New York Jets vs. Buffalo Bills—
September 26, 1965

America is truly the land of opportunity. Any boy entering high school today has a good chance of getting a college education and then going on to acquire "all the good things in life"—a big bank account, an expensive car, a jazzy big city apartment, and a little address book containing the names of two dozen pretty girls, all waiting anxiously at the telephone for his call. There is only one prerequisite: he must make his mark early in football, baseball, or basketball.

Joe Namath took no chances: he starred in all three sports. He might have gone directly from high school to a career in baseball if his mother hadn't insisted he get a college degree first. No member of the Namath family had such a precious hunk of parchment paper, and Mrs. Namath wanted her Joe Willie to be the first. To the lean, muscular kid, that was practically a command. He ended up at Alabama.

In his three years with the varsity football team, Namath took the Crimson Tide through three winning seasons. In fact, the number three crops up all the way through his scholastic career. He played three years, Alabama lost only three games during that time, and the team played in three bowl games. Note that the *team*, not Joe Willie, appeared three times. During his junior year, he broke training after the regular season was over, even though he knew Alabama was slated to play in the Sugar Bowl against Mississippi. Coach Bear Bryant promptly suspended him from the squad. By then Namath was so popular in the state that Bryant —the only football personality in Alabama more popular than Joe Willie Namath—had to go on television to explain why the young passer was barred from playing.

Joe ended his college career in a blaze of glory. Alabama was ranked first in the nation by the Associated Press and the United Press International. Yet Namath was sidelined a good part of the time. In the fourth game of the season, playing against North Carolina, he hurt his knee. Fortunately, the Crimson Tide had a sub quarterback named Steve Sloan who would have been good enough to be a first stringer on most other college teams. Sloan did quite well, but it was Namath's spot-playing that pulled a couple of key games out of the fire. Against Georgia Tech and Auburn, Joe tossed touchdown passes which put those games into the win column for the Crimson Tide. He ended the year with a sixty-four percent completion record to lead the Southeast Conference.

Furthermore, his knee had improved, although he knew an operation was necessary if he were to play pro football.

Oh, they wanted Namath, and the bids were in early. The Jets especially were ready to shell out a fortune for him. The New York scouting report on him read, "Best passing quarterback in the South . . . a great passer . . . GET HIM!"

Disaster almost overtook Namath during practice for the Orange Bowl game against tough Texas. He was practicing hand-offs, twisting sharply to transfer the ball. Nobody was coming in at him and nobody touched him. Suddenly there was a loud "pop" that could be heard all over the field. Namath went hobbling off the field. The knee was packed in ice, and the doctor's gloomy report indicated that Joe would be out of action for ten days—which meant no Orange Bowl for him.

With Namath seemingly lost, all attention turned to backup man Steve Sloan. But now he was also a questionable starter, for he had pulled ligaments in his knee. He could play, but Bryant had been counting on a healthy Namath to take over. With both quarterbacks on gimpy legs, Bryant was in a bad way. Only two others on the Crimson Tide team *might* be installed as replacements: Wayne Trimble, a sophomore running back, and Buddy French, the punter. They had worked out at the position to back up Sloan when Namath was hurt. However, when Namath showed he could return to action during the season, both had returned to their original duties.

Joe Willie Namath wasn't about to let a "little thing" like a popped knee keep him out of the Orange Bowl. After taking two days of ultrasonic and ice-pack treatments, he was back on the practice field. The knee seemed to be holding up to some degree. But during the game Namath had trouble setting up for the pass. He was a step slower. The charging defense had that extra time to get a crack at him.

Furthermore, the Longhorns had just the man to come busting through. All-American linebacker Tommy Nobis was already a "can't miss" pro prospect (he went on to the Atlanta Falcons after college); and if Nobis got to Namath, he'd bend that bad leg into a very interesting geometric shape.

There were others on the Texas team who could give any team in the country a very bad time. Carrying the mail was Ernie Koy, Jr., son of the old-time outfielder of the Brooklyn Dodgers. At end was George Sauer, Jr., son of one of the New York Jets coaches. Eventually both men played in New York: Koy with the New York Giants, and Sauer with the Jets, where he became one of Joe Willie's favorite targets.

The Texas team was fifth-ranked in the nation. Only once had they dropped a game, and that one to Arkansas. Trailing 14-7, the Longhorns had pushed over another touchdown and trailed 14-13. A place-kick conversion would have tied the score, but Royal wanted a win. He didn't get it as the attempt at a 2-point conversion failed.

When the game started, Texas was the underdog, in spite of Alabama's two hobbling quarterbacks. Steve Bowman was the reason the Tide was considered tough. He was a dandy running back, one of the best in the conference.

Some 73,000 fans jammed the Orange Bowl and saw a comparatively quiet game during most of the first quarter. Alabama got a break when a Texas fumble was recovered by the Tide on the Longhorn 41, but Sloan couldn't move the team.

The period was just about over when the real action started. Texas had the ball on its own 21, and Ernie

75

Koy took a pitchout. He cut over right tackle, saw daylight and opened the throttle. On the 40 he picked up a key block that wiped out the Alabama safety man, and after that no one came near him. It was a 79-yard scamper, an Orange Bowl record run from scrimmage.

Darrell Royal had taught his boys to protect a lead, to play sound, ball-control conservative football once they got out in front. So, after Alabama's Dave Ray tried a field goal and missed, to leave the Tide 7 points behind, Royal sent in his sub quarterback, Jim Hudson. Bryant knew that he'd see a running game for a while. It turned out that way—for a couple of plays anyway. And it was those *little* mistakes that cost Alabama dearly.

When Texas couldn't do much on three plays, Koy went back to punt. He did. But Alabama was offside, so the Longhorns found themselves still in possession, with a first down on their own 31.

So Hudson called a pass play. He waited until Sauer got behind safety man Mickey Andrews. Sauer gathered it in on the 'Bama 22 and practically jogged the rest of the way. Now it was 14-0, Texas.

That was more than Namath could take. He'd been warming the bench—Joe had entered the game for only one play—and the way things looked, the Tide couldn't do much worse with him in the lineup.

Some players have the innate ability to fire up a team with just their physical presence. Joe Willie Namath is just such a man. With the stringbean quarterback calling the signals, Alabama got moving in a hurry. Starting on their own 13, the team began to forge steadily ahead toward the Texas goal line. They went winging in on Namath's arm. It took 14 plays, and 81 of the 87 yards were eaten up by passes. Ten times he threw, and six of the throws were caught. One went astray and three others hit the receivers right in the hands but were dropped. The pay dirt pitch was a 3-yarder to half-back Wayne Trimble. Score: Texas 14, Alabama 7.

Back came Texas with its own drive, which stalled on the Alabama 28. They set up for a field goal on the 35, and 'Bama braced. As the ball was spotted down, the forward wall came busting through. Then came one of those heart-breaking plays that can deflate all the momentum built up by a team.

The kick was blocked. An Alabama player picked it up, and then he fumbled. Texas recovered on the Alabama 38.

The Longhorns cashed in on the break. Two passes from Hudson to Sauer put the ball on the 1-foot line, and Ernie Koy took it across. Texas had its two-touchdown lead back again. A mere seventeen seconds later the gun ended the half.

Joe Willie Namath was far from through. The next time Alabama got its hands on the ball, he started them grinding it out again. The key play in the drive showed the courage and determination of this kid named Namath. It was fourth down with 8 yards to go on the Texas 38. Namath went for it. He drilled one to Ray Perkins, who was downed on the 20. The next play was another pass to Perkins, and that one was over the goal line. It had been a 9-play, 63-yard march. Now it was 21-14, Texas.

Six seconds into the fourth quarter the Tide had scored again. This one capped a drive that saw the team go 60 yards, and 31 of those yards were the result of three Namath passes. When the march bogged down,

Dave Ray kicked a field goal. Strangely, it was the same angle he had missed back in the first period. Ray had caught fire, too.

Leading now by only four points, Texas tried to add an insurance touchdown. But Jim Fuller, the Alabama tackle, intercepted a pass out in the flat, and the Tide had another chance. They moved to the 6, first and goal, as the stands erupted in a frenzy of screaming. Three times Steve Bowman hurled himself into the line, and three times he failed to make it as the Texas line turned to granite. On fourth down Namath kept the ball on a quarterback sneak. The teams piled up around the goal line. When they untangled, the referee signaled no! Joe Willie had been stopped on the 6-inch line!

Texas wedged out of trouble and then punted out to the Alabama 31. The clock showed two minutes thirteen seconds left to play as Namath returned to the attack. A pass to Ogden was good to the Texas 41, and the noise from the crowd could be heard for miles. Namath missed the next try. A penalty set Alabama back 5 yards. Namath tried and missed. Namath tried and missed. Namath tried and missed. They lost the ball. Texas ran out the clock. Final score: Texas 21, Alabama 17.

It had been a tremendous performance by Joe Willie Namath. Playing with a bad leg, jeopardizing his future pro career, he had nevertheless showed why he was rated the number-one passer in the country. He had completed 18 of 37 for 255 yards and two touchdowns. And he had been throwing without setting up while he was off balance, falling away. Yet with a simple flick of those steel-cabled wrists he whipped the ball 40 and 50 yards to his receivers, right on the button. One of his tosses, a 37-yarder that might have won the game, was dropped in the end zone. Nobody even blinked when the Orange Bowl's Most Valuable Player award was handed to Joe Namath.

The young man from Beaver Falls, Pennsylvania, had played that game for more than glory. It was really a "show me" game. The papers had printed reams of copy regarding his signing with the Jets for $400,000. Everyone who saw him in action agreed he had been cheap at the price.

The knee operation was performed during the winter, and the medics assured Sonny Werblin and Weeb Ewbank that the leg was sound again. There would be some pain and stiffness, but if Namath went through the prescribed series of vigorous exercises to strengthen the knee, it would definitely respond. And that happened, too.

Yet the rookie was far from sure of a regular job. With a great deal of additional fanfare, the Jets had also signed Heisman Trophy winner Johnny Huarte, the Notre Dame quarterback, and shelled out $200,000 to get him. In addition the team already had Mike Taliaferro listed as the starting quarterback, and Taliaferro was out to prove that the team really didn't need $600,000 worth of passers while he was around. It turned out that he was right.

Johnny Huarte was slated to play in the August all-star game, meaning he'd miss a lot of practice with the Jets, and rookie quarterbacks just can't do that and expect to catch up later on. And Namath found out, in practice and during the exhibition season, that pro defenses were a lot tougher to read than college defenses. He made mistakes, a lot of them.

But there was one skill in his arsenal of passing talents that nobody in the AFL could match: he had the quickest release in the league. Once he set up to throw, that ball was gone. Other passers seemed to be working in slow motion by comparison as they cocked their arms, shifted their weight, and let it fly. With Namath it was one quick, fluid motion; he'd backpedal, ball held chest high, and then stop—and the next instant it was spiraling away like a rifle bullet. He threw from behind his ear with a quick wrist flip, like a baseball catcher pegging the ball to second base.

However, Namath wasn't ready to start a game, and since Huarte no longer figured in the picture, Mike Taliaferro was the only choice left. Namath was on the sidelines manning the telephone.

Taliaferro wasn't exactly overpowering, and the Jets lost the first two. It wasn't so much the losses that bothered Ewbank—although in pro football losing a game is akin to a federal offense—as it was the dispirited play of the Jets. They looked sluggish, uninspired. The coach decided to start Joe Willie. He certainly couldn't do worse than lose, and he might even show some promise. Besides, New York fans were beginning to wonder if the $400,000 flash were ever going to get into a ball game for any length of time. They had been brainwashed into thinking he was potentially another Johnny Unitas; so where was he?

On September 26, 1965, Joe Willie Namath was in the starting lineup. And during the early part of the game the Jets might just as well have started Taliaferro, because the club went nowhere. It was Buffalo's Jackie Kemp who kept connecting with his throws. While the Bills' fans watched gleefully, Kemp engineered drives, one after the other, resulting in one touchdown and two field goals by soccer-style kicker Pete Gogolak. Buffalo had a 13-0 lead when the Jets suddenly came alive.

The New York scoring started when a Jet march slowed and Jim Turner kicked a field goal to make it 13-3. A minute later the Jets recovered a fumble, and that was when Namath unlimbered the good right arm.

A fast pass to Matt Snell coming out of the backfield was good for 33 yards, and then a flip to Billy Mathis in the end zone got the touchdown. Things were definitely looking up when the Jets went into the dressing room at halftime trailing by only 13-10.

The second half turned into a corking passing duel between Kemp and Namath. Kemp—who had been rejected by the National Football League because he threw too hard(!)—got the Bills another touchdown and a pair of field goals. Namath got the touchdown back; he hit flanker Don Maynard with a 30-yarder, and then hit him again for 25 more. He switched over to tight end Dee Mackey and that one went for 9 yards and the TD. This rookie could really heave that football!

Joe Willie wasn't content with an ordinary conversion. He went for the 2-pointer, and he got it with a pass. Score: Buffalo 26, New York 18.

Midway through the fourth quarter Joe Willie masterminded a Jet drive that began on the New York 21. He handed off, he passed short, and the Jets were on the Buffalo 16; but the club ran out of gas. It was fourth down, and the yardage needed for a first down was long and tough to get.

There were still five minutes to play. A field goal would put the Jets into a position where another TD could pull out the game, provided the Jet defense could hold. The field goal looked like good strategy. The Jets got it with Jim Turner's leg.

That was when Buffalo rose to the occasion. Kemp and the Bills ground out the first downs one at a time, eating up the clock, and just before the gun went off they had another touchdown. Final score: Buffalo 33, Jets 21.

But that lost ball game had proved Joe Willie Namath to be a comer indeed. He had completed 19 passes, and Taliaferro had needed two games to do that. He had been blitzed unmercifully by the hard-charging Buffalo defense and had come through unscathed. And, best of all, he was the kind of field leader who could pick up the team when the breaks were going bad, and he could make them come back.

The rest of the story is almost too well known to repeat. Joe Willie Namath was the AFL Rookie of the Year and finished third in passing. Every opposing coach and every defensive lineman in the league agreed that he was on his way to being one of the best, if not eventually *the* best.

There had been many doubting Thomases among the fans when the Jets first went after Joe Willie. He made believers out of them all with just two games: in the Orange Bowl against Texas, and in his first start against a pro team. Strangely, his team lost both times!

You Need a Quarterback to Win

Green Bay Packers vs. Baltimore Colts—
December 26, 1965

Back in 1963, the New York Giants didn't have much in the way of a running attack. Joe Morrison was a versatile halfback in that he could move the ball and catch a pass and could rate a spot somewhere on any National Football League team. Phil King was adequate as a fullback. He could plunge ahead to pick up the couple of yards fullbacks are called upon to make. But there was no break-away runner, no big threat to go all the way. New York's ground game was weak.

However, the Giants did have a quarterback named Yelberton Abraham Tittle. "Yat," they called him, or "the Bald Eagle," or "Colonel Slick." And he broke a lot of passing records that year, so the Giants won the Eastern Division title.

Now, a football team needs a lot more than a quarterback to make it a winner. There are such fundamentals as defense, passer protection, and at least the threat of a line plunge or two, if for no other reason than to keep the other guys honest. But still, the quarterback is the core of the team, the one who makes the machine tick. Even with all the other plus values a team must have—the defense and the ground game—a good quarterback spells the difference between the championship and ending up in second or third place.

For a time during the 1965 season the Baltimore Colts seemed to have everything. Their running was fine, defense top notch, and as for quarterbacking, they had the best in the business: Johnny Unitas.

Anyone who has ever seen a game of pro football or talked to a fan has heard the name Johnny Unitas. His name is mentioned weekly, at any game, regardless of which teams are playing. Because when Johnny U was in his prime, there was simply nobody better. Not anyone! This product of the Pennsylvania coal districts, who was turned down by three different pro teams and had to play semi-pro football before being discovered—why, he could paste a piece of thread onto the point of a football and then throw it right through a needle, ball and all! He made the Colts' offensive engine purr like a catnipped kitten. But when he wasn't there—trouble!

The 1965 season was a case in point. The Colts started out as if there were no such word as "defeat" in any dictionary. They peeled off seven victories in a row and tied the eighth game. But in the Chicago game Unitas was belted down hard and his knee went out. He was through for the season.

Fortunately, the Colts had a young backup man named Gary Cuozzo, considered by some to be the best second-string quarterback in the NFL. The kid tried hard to fill Johnny U's shoes, but that was like asking a batting practice pitcher to take over for the Mets' Tom Seaver. Cuozzo did well enough, but the Colts lost a couple of tough ones. Still, the game of December 12 gave Baltimore a chance to slip off with the Western Division championship if they could only get by the Green Bay Packers, who were closing the gap fast. But the Packers would go into first place by half a game if they won.

Since Unitas had been injured, leaving Baltimore with only one quarterback, coach Don Shula had halfback Tom Matte work out at the signal-calling spot. Matte had played the position some in college, but was no passer. He was strictly on call for emergencies only.

For a while it was a tight game, and there was a moment when it seemed that the breaks were favoring Baltimore and that they would manage to knock off Green Bay, even without Unitas.

The Packers were ahead, 14-13. But a fumble deep in their own territory had given Baltimore the ball and the Colts were on the Green Bay 2-yard line. The play that followed proved to be the turning point.

Cuozzo faked a handoff to Lenny Moore, who plunged into the line. At the same time fullback Jerry Hill went to the outside and cut into the end zone as a pass receiver. But defensive end Willie Davis and linebacker Dave Robinson had smelled out the play (later Davis said one of the Baltimore offensive linemen tipped off the play by the way he adjusted his feet before the ball was snapped. Smart cookies, these pro players!). Instead of moving inward to choke off Moore's fake rush, they fell off to cover Hill. Cuozzo's toss was high and soft. Davis leaped and the ball grazed his fingertips; Robinson cut in behind him, in front of Hill, and grabbed it. Then the linebacker chugged 88 yards to the Baltimore 10-yard line. Green

Bay scored again. Instead of going out in front, Baltimore had to play catch-up football, and that's hard to do against the Packers.

Probably the Colts wouldn't have won anyway, for Green Bay's superlative halfback, Paul "Golden Boy" Hornung, chose that afternoon to run wild and score five touchdowns.

And, as if the loss of the game—and the loss of the league lead—weren't bad enough, Baltimore suffered still a third setback: Cuozzo was hurt! He managed to play a bit more in the game after being shot full of pain killer, but afterward his banged-up shoulder was taped and his arm put in a sling. He joined Johnny Unitas on the sidelines.

And now the Baltimore Colts had no quarterback at all!

The Colts were desperate. Tom Matte was a willing worker but not much of a passer; he could throw about as well as most football players can when they're fooling around, tossing the ball back and forth. Yet he was all they had. And, to their consternation, he suddenly came down with a case of sniffles. At first it was feared that he had contracted influenza, but it proved to be a slight cold. Still, the Colts needed someone else as backup for Matte.

Healthy first-class pro quarterbacks—even second stringers—have always been in short supply in pro football. Baltimore shopped around, and the only one they could come up with was Ed Brown of the Pittsburgh Steelers.

Brown had seen his best days; in fact, even the Steelers seldom used him. Mostly he held the ball for the place kicker on field goal and point-after-touchdown attempts. Throughout the season he had appeared in only three games as passer. He'd attempted 18 and completed 7, which certainly wasn't much of a record. But Baltimore was glad to get anybody, especially at the $100 waiver price. As one of the Steeler officials said later, "Well, maybe Baltimore will remember us in their will for our present to them."

Baltimore still had an outside chance to regain the Division lead. The team had one more game to play, against the Los Angeles Rams. Normally, with a healthy Unitas (or even a Cuozzo for that matter) the Colts would have creamed Los Angeles, for the Rams were far down in the standings and had been losing consistently through most of the season. But now, with the Colts using a running back and a reject to lead them, the Rams figured to take the ball game. Brown had worked out for a few days with Baltimore, but he still wasn't familiar with the offensive plays.

Baltimore led at the half, 10-7. Mostly it was the defense that kept the Colts ahead, as Dennis Gaubatz and Steve Stonebreaker put the pressure on the Ram passing attack. Los Angeles had also lost its first-string passer, Bill Munson, who had been hurt in a previous game. But Roman Gabriel was the Rams starter, and having him in the lineup was no great hardship.

Gabriel showed his stuff when action resumed. Guiding the team skillfully, he engineered a drive downfield, capped by a scoring touchdown. A field goal was added to the total and the Rams went ahead, 17-10 in the fourth quarter. Baltimore needed some scores fast, or the end of the game would also mark the end of the season for them.

They needed the long bomb, the yard-eating pass. That meant Brown would have to be used, since Matte couldn't throw for distance.

What followed should only have happened in a game played by twenty-year-olds on a pickup team. Coach Don Shula knelt and, with some of his offensive players grouped around, drew a diagram on the sidelines, using a stick for a pencil and the ground itself for a blackboard. Then, with Baltimore on its own 32, Brown took the snap, dropped back, and let his protection form. He waited until the last possible second before lofting the ball high and far. Tight end John Mackey sprinted along the sidelines, turned, took the ball in full stride and continued across the last chalk mark. The conversion was added and Baltimore had tied the game at 17-all!

The stout defense stopped Los Angeles, and Baltimore started another late drive. Matte was in there leading the team, and it was a ground attack all the way. Mostly it was Matte himself carrying, using draw plays, keepers, and rollouts as he bit off chunks of yardage: 14 yards, 10 yards, 20 yards. In 13 plays they were in position for a field goal from the 23. Lou Michaels put it through with his toe and Baltimore had a 20-17 edge.

The Rams tried to strike back, and for a time it seemed they'd go all the way. In the last minute of play Bobby Boyd intercepted a Gabriel pass dangerously near his own goal line, and that killed the rally.

If the surprise 68-yard pass play were not counted, Baltimore had won the game without a passing attack. Only seven passes had been tried and three completed, counting the scoring toss from Brown to Mackey. Tom Matte had attempted two and completed none; Brown went 3-for-5. All the rest had been running plays.

YOU NEED A QUARTERBACK TO WIN

The Rams-Colts clash was a Saturday game. Green Bay was to play the San Francisco 49ers the following afternoon. Since Baltimore had already played and won, they were in sole possession of the Western Division lead by half a game. But if the Packers beat the 49ers, Green Bay would be champs of the Division. And that seemed to be in the cards, for the 49ers were no great shakes, having won seven and lost six during the season.

As Baltimore players watched the game on television, chewing their fingernails down to the nub, the Packers took a 24-17 lead into the final minute and seven seconds of play. Then San Francisco quarterback John Brodie hit Vern Burke with a twenty-seven-yard touchdown heave, and when Tommy Davis calmly place-kicked the extra point, the teams were tied. So Green Bay didn't take home the title—at least not that day.

Now Baltimore and Green Bay had identical records: 10 won, 3 lost, 1 tied. The teams would have to engage in a playoff game to settle the Divisional championship. All the rules of championship play were to be in force, including "sudden death overtime" in case the game ended in a tie at the end of regulation time.

It was windy and cold the day after Christmas when the Pack and the Colts met for the divisional title. The stands were filled. Both teams were up for the game. If either lost, that would be the end of them. There was no tomorrow.

The game wasn't thirty seconds old when the first break turned all strategy upside down!

Green Bay brought the kickoff out to the 15-yard line. The Pack's ace passer, Bart Starr, planned to grab the initiative right away, and he called for a pass to his tight end, Bill Anderson. The pass was completed all right, but

Baltimore's Lenny Lyles banged into Anderson so hard that he fumbled. Don Shinnick picked up the ball and tore down the sidelines. Starr cut over to stop the play. Near the goal, Jim Welch, who was running interference for Shinnick, threw a hard, clean block into the Green Bay passer, knocking him back a full five feet. Shinnick scored; Starr lay where he fell. He was helped into the locker room where his injury was described as badly bruised ribs. Starr was out of action, at least insofar as passing was concerned.

Green Bay's backup man, Zeke Bratkowski—nicknamed "the Brat," although he was thirty-three years old—took over the reins. He couldn't get the Pack moving in the first period. Baltimore couldn't do much either. In the second quarter the Colts managed a drive to the Green Bay 7 but were stopped. Lou Michaels put the ball over the crossbar, and Baltimore led by 10-0.

The Packers came back with a drive of their own and soon were knocking on the Colts' door. Green Bay had a second down, a yard to go on the Baltimore final hash mark. Actually, the ball was even closer to the goal, and some onlookers said it was on the 6-inch line.

A smash at the line went exactly no place, and the ball was spotted down on exactly the same piece of turf.

Everyone in the stands and everyone watching the game on television knew who'd carry the ball on the final plunge: the hard-nosed, contact-relishing, slugging fullback, Jim Taylor. That's what happened. Bratkowski fed him the ball and Taylor went into the right side of the line. Lou Michaels hit him first, throwing his own body in Taylor's path to stop him from advancing. Then Dennis Gaubatz rammed into the Packer fullback, spinning him around like a top and shoving him back. The ball popped out of Taylor's arms; he fell on it, but yardage was lost. Baltimore had put on a great goal-line stand and took over on downs. The half ended with the Colts still leading by 10-0.

Into the third period went the teams, alternately pushing and shoving across midfield, but not getting very far. It would take a few good breaks for either side to do much. Baltimore had already felt the glow of Lady Luck's smile. Now it was Green Bay's turn.

In the third period, in a punt situation for Baltimore, the snap from center was bad and Green Bay got the ball on Baltimore's 35. They ground out the yardage until the 1-yard line was reached again. This time Paul Hornung punched in for the tally.

There was no more scoring in the period, and the clubs battled into the final quarter with Green Bay still trailing. Late in the period the Packers began moving the ball again and reached the 15 where the attack stalled. With two minutes left on the clock, Don Chandler connected for a 22-yard field goal to tie the score. Then time ran out.

The sudden-death fifth period began, and still nobody had the muscle to go far. But now Green Bay's varied attack was beginning to get them better field position. Tom Matte was directing the Colts, and he wasn't a passing threat; Green Bay knew that, so they played short, looking for the ground game. Matte tried 12 passes during that game and completed only 5; all were short ones. He racked up only 40 yards passing all day. Yet he gained 57 yards running with the ball!

Again, late in the extra period, Green Bay started to grind out the yardage until they were inside the Baltimore 20. They could go no farther. So, in the gathering gloom,

Don Chandler was called upon. From the 25 his kick sailed up and over. The Packers were champs!

It had taken the vaunted Green Bay team thirteen minutes and thirty-nine seconds of overtime to beat a determined team which had no first string and no backup quarterback. However, the Packers had been going without their own first-stringer throughout almost the entire game. Second-guessers tried to figure out what *might* have happened under various sets of different circumstances:

Suppose Johnny U had been healthy and Bart Starr wasn't hurt? Would the teams have battled so evenly? Possibly.

Suppose Cuozzo hadn't been injured? Could he have led the Colt attack differently against Bratkowski's leadership? Who knows?

What if Starr and Bratkowski had both been racked up in that game, and Green Bay had to call on somebody else—possibly Paul Hornung, who had once been the Pack's passer? Maybe Green Bay would have lost by a wide margin.

It's all conjecture anyway, and no one will ever know what *might* have happened. But those last games proved one thing conclusively: in pro football, a team can't win very often without a good passer.

The Money Players

*Green Bay Packers vs. Baltimore Colts—
December 10, 1966;*

*Green Bay Packers vs. Dallas Cowboys—
January 1, 1967*

In the world of professional athletics, the term "money player" refers to the man who wins the big match, the important game, the crucial contest that leads to the big money. When two teams are fighting it out for the whole ball of wax, the better club doesn't necessarily come out on top. It's the team that will fight harder, or capitalize on the unexpected break before the stunned victims can regroup and come back, or make its own break by forcing the opposition into mistakes. Call it desire, or opportunism, or even pride; somehow, the money players will find a way to win.

The next question is, what happens when two sets of money players collide head-on?

The answer is that there's no way to figure the outcome. Sometimes an entire ball game can hinge on one play, a half-yard that couldn't be gained because somebody slipped and fell, a fumble, a missed catch, a bad punt, a broken shoelace, a missed block. And that split second can spell the difference between the champion's slice of the cake and the crumbs left over for the also-rans.

Back in 1966, the one player who could be classified as *the* money player of pro football was Baltimore's dandy little quarterback, Johnny Unitas. This guy had everything—desire, ability, experience, and a talent for leadership. As long as Johnny U was on the firing line, the Colts couldn't be counted out of a ball game until all the players were in their street clothes and the ushers were sweeping out the stands. He proved he deserved the number-one rating, pulling off so many clutch plays that nobody bothered to count them any longer. Unitas was often dubbed "Icewater Johnny," a passer with "the guts of a burglar." Most quarterbacks fall victim to the occupational hazard known as "the patter of little feet." Almost subconsciously they begin to hear the hoofbeats in the thundering herd—the front fours and the linebackers—blitzing in, and they begin to cringe in their cleats. Not Johnny U. He'd stand there in the passing cup, ignoring those 275-pound ends and tackles until the last possible moment, and then he'd throw the football. On the receiving end of the passes were the fine old pros, such as Ray Berry, Willie Richardson, Lennie Moore, Jimmy Orr, and the burly tight end, John Mackey.

The Green Bay Packers were also loaded with that breed: offensive guard Jerry Kramer, end Max McGee, and quarterback Ray Nitschke, defensive back Herb Adderley, and quarterback Bart Starr. All had made a habit of winning the big games. Sure, they lost a few during the regular season, but not the important ones; never the games that counted big.

Unfortunately, Baltimore hadn't had *that* good a season. Most of the year they had chased Green Bay, and with two games left on the schedule, they trailed the Pack by two. If Green Bay lost both and if Baltimore won both, they would end in a tie. As it happened, the Colts had a chance to do something, because the next-to-last game for both was a head-to-head meeting between them.

Neither of these "money playing" teams could foresee that the outcome of the clash would hinge on one crucial play.

Some 60,000 fans paid their way into Baltimore's Memorial Stadium to watch a fairly routine game of football played during a dreary afternoon of intermittent rain. Johnny U wasn't up to par that day, for he was nursing a painfully sore shoulder; but he hung in there, giving the Colts all he had, and that was plenty.

Green Bay got on the scoreboard in the first frame. Defensive back Willie Wood intercepted an errant Unitas throw to give the Packers possession. Starr capitalized on the break with the help of running back Elijah Pitts. The quarterback sent Pitts straight out of the backfield; Pitts split defenders Jerry Logan and Alvin Haymond, took the pass and slithered home. The play covered 42 yards.

Fate returned the break to Baltimore with interest during the next quarter. Unitas found Tom Matte with a 24-yarder that carried to the Packer 4. A couple of plays later, Tony Lorick followed a devastating block by Jim Parker and went over from the 1. The kick tied the score.

The kickoff that followed was dropped by Donny Anderson, and the Colts recovered. The Pack front four shut off any gains, and Lou Michaels toed the ball over from the 26. Baltimore led at the half by 10-7.

Green Bay had every reason to feel dispirited as they went to the locker room to rub some of the mud off their bodies. Not only were they losing, but also they had to forgo the services of Bart Starr, who sustained an injury shortly before the second period ended. For the rest of the game the burden would fall on the creaking shoulders of thirty-four-year-old Zeke Bratkowski, the Pack's backup passer. Zeke was unspectacular, but generally he managed to get the job done. However, the experts didn't figure they would do too well in the mud and puddles with a second-stringer directing traffic.

But strangely enough the Packers themselves never doubted for a moment they'd win. They didn't have to beat Baltimore to take the title; even a tie was okay. Or they could win the next one, and Baltimore might drop their finale. Any combination of possibilities was good enough. But there was Packer pride at stake. They didn't want to back into the title if they could possibly help it. Money players don't operate that way.

The teams struggled through a scoreless third quarter and into the final period. The Pack could have tied the game on three different occasions, but each time the usually reliable Don Chandler missed his field goal attempts, once from only 29 yards out.

Finally "the Brat" got the club moving. Starting from his own 20, he led his mates through ten plays into scoring land. The key play was a third-and-7 call from the Colt 25, when old Zeke hung the ball out to veteran Max McGee and the Packer end was downed on Baltimore's 4. In practically no time Elijah Pitts went across behind great blocking by guards Jerry Kramer and Forrest Gregg. Green Bay led, 14-10.

Still nobody counted the Colts out, because Johnny U had started the wheels turning again. As the clock continued to run, he took the underdog Baltimore team steadily over the soggy turf, and there they were on the Green Bay 16 with a first down. The dripping Baltimore rooters were seeing a true money player at his very best!

There were eighty-nine seconds left as Unitas called for a pass. He took the snap and dropped back. Green Bay's defense spread out, covering every available Baltimore receiver. And there was a gaping hole right up the middle. With that peculiar lope of his, Johnny U took out straight for the Packer goal line.

Defensive end Willie Davis, the nine-year all-pro from Grambling, applied the brakes to his own charge and went circling back. At the 9-yard line, just as it seemed that Unitas was going all the way, Davis reached out a ham-like hand and grabbed at Johnny U's arm. Unitas was carrying the ball high, tucked under the crook of his right arm. Davis made contact, hitting Unitas with part of his body, and with his hand he tore at Johnny's arm which held the ball. He wasn't content merely to stop the high-stepping quarterback; he had to force a fumble. And that was what happened! The ball popped away; linebacker Dave Robinson fell on it. And five plays later the ball game was over.

It wasn't one of Green Bay's better efforts. In fact, they came within a hair's breadth of losing the game, because if Davis had skidded or slipped just a fraction, or even if he had merely made the tackle, Unitas would simply have called time out and therefore had a chance to run two, three, or four more plays, and possibly even pulled the game out. But money player Davis came up with the big play, the smart play, the money play.

So Green Bay had the divisional championship, and on January 1 they bumped heads with the Dallas Cowboys to see who would become champs of the whole National

Football League. It was almost like a set of twins having a family fight, because the two teams were so much alike that it was almost laughable.

Both had marvelous front fours, standout sets of linebackers, and pretty good defensive backs. In fact, Dallas had led its division in defense, yielding only 239 points. They had also led in offense with 445 points scored. Likewise, Green Bay led in defense, allowing a mere 163 points, and they were also divisional scoring leaders, racking up 335 points. Don Meredith was a seasoned veteran of the MFL wars—some said the equal of Bart Starr. And he had at his disposal "the world's fastest human," Olympic sprinter Bob Hayes, awaiting his passing pleasure. Oh, yes, this was a money team too.

Green Bay showed that it was in no mood to fool around: the Pack took the opening kickoff and chewed out 76 yards in a mere eight plays from scrimmage. The score came on a 17-yard pass to Elijah Pitts.

Seconds later Vince Lombardi's boys doubled their total. Mel Renfro of the Cowboys fumbled the kickoff; Jim Grabowski picked up the ball on the 19 and lost no time running home with it. The 75,000 fans at the Cotton Bowl had barely opened their programs and already Green Bay led by two touchdowns.

Other teams might have folded up and died, but not Dallas. Don Meredith had two hard-running backs in Dan Reeves and Don Perkins, and he put them to work as soon as Dallas got the ball back. The result was two sustained drives: one covered 65 yards and ended in a touchdown by Reeves, the other in a 23-yard romp by Perkins for the tie-score touchdown.

All that action happened in the first quarter! Up to that point Bart Starr had been keeping his passes short.

The Dallas secondary were expecting him to keep them that way, so he double-crossed them with a beauty to flanker Carroll Dale that started on Green Bay's 49 and wound up 51 yards away with Dale sprinting in for the score.

Meredith and the Cowboys didn't take that lying down and came right back, chewing out nice chunks of yardage with their running game. When the backs were stopped, Danny Villanueva got a field goal from the 11. The half ended with Green Bay hanging on to a 21-17 edge.

Soon after the second half opened, that margin was cut to a single point as Villanueva kicked another 3-pointer. It was turning out to be a strange kind of game. Green Bay, known for its ball-control type of offense, couldn't run against that big Dallas line and had to resort to passes in order to get anywhere. Dallas, which had speedy Bob Hayes as wide receiver, was having less luck in the air but could pick up ground by running. That was pointed up even more when, later in the quarter, Starr hit Boyd Dowler with a 16-yard scoring strike, his third touchdown pass of the day. The Pack couldn't get close enough to the goal to carry the ball across on the ground.

In the fourth quarter Starr struck again, this time with a 28-yard pass to Max McGee. On paper Green Bay was running up a big score. But a sharp observer could see that the Green Bay offensive line was running out of gas and that before too long the Dallas front four was going to make merry with Kramer, Gregg, et al. There were very definite signs of collapse:

a) As Starr was dropping back for his third-period touchdown pass to Dowler, Cowboy linebacker Chuck Howley came busting through the pass pocket. He dove, reached out, and grabbed Starr by the ankles. The Packer passer was actually falling down when he threw the football, but managed to lay it right in Dowler's lap.

b) In the fourth quarter, before he found McGee open, Starr was constantly confronted by impossible situations. They say that football is a game of third-down plays, and on three occasions Starr had to overcome big losses. The first time it was third down, 19 to go; the second time it was third down, 12 to go; the third time it was third down, 19 to go. Yet somehow that money player named Bart Starr got the first down every time!

c) Furthermore, the try for the extra point on that last touchdown failed, because six-foot, five-inch Bob Lilly came in, stuck out his arm, and blocked the conversion try.

So the Pack led by 34-20, and it looked like the end of a very average game of football—except that Tom Landry's team wasn't convinced the game was over. Don Meredith proved there were still at least a few good minutes left in the Cowboys, for he collaborated with Frank Clarke on a gorgeous 68-yard touchdown pass. And when Danny Villanueva's kick was good, that Lilly-blocked conversion loomed large indeed, for the Cowboys could still tie the game with just one more scoring play.

Now came the opportunity to see what true money players can do when everything is riding on one minute of football!

Fighting tenaciously, refusing to give ground, the Dallas Cowboys stopped Green Bay's attempt to run out the clock with ground plays. Don Chandler got off a weak punt that traveled only 16 yards. And there was Dallas with the football on the Packer 47 with two and a half minutes remaining. Why, that was all the time in the world!

Since Clarke had been his lucky charm, Meredith went back to him, and the pass clicked for 21 yards. Pressing his luck, Dandy Don stuck with Clarke and heaved one in his direction again. The receiver was wide open as the ball sailed toward him. There was only one thing safety man Tom Brown could do, and that was to shove him away from the path of the football. It was flagrant interference, and the ref's flag was on the ground while Clarke was still teetering to keep his balance. He gave the Cowboys the ball on the Green Bay 2, first and goal to go.

The delirious Cowboy crowd was on its feet to a man as Dan Reeves bucked into the line for a yard. The cheers turned to groans as Dallas was offside and set back to the 6. Reeves dropped a pass, but another Meredith toss was good back to the 2-yard line. Fourth down, goal to go. And once again it all boiled down to a single play. If the Cowboys made it, the game would go into overtime, and if that happened, the team surely had the momentum to stop the wilting Packer drives, get the ball back, and grab an overtime victory. But if they failed. . . .

In the huddle Meredith called for a play known as "Fire 90." The quarterback rolled out and, if a receiver was open, he threw it; if not, he kept it and went on his own.

But Dave Robinson, the Packer linebacker, saw it coming. He slipped in and grabbed Meredith. The Cowboy passer threw anyway, but it was a wobbly toss and Tom Brown intercepted. The game was over.

So—what is a money player? It's Johnny Unitas running across a muddy football field in the last seconds of a game, almost snatching victory away from the favored team. And it's Willie Davis chasing him, grabbing his arm, forcing a fumble so that his team could nail down the lid on the divisional title.

A money player is Don Meredith crossing up the opposition by throwing to the same receiver three times and making each pass count. And it's a great linebacker named Dave Robinson—tired, bruised, and still making the big play. And it's Bart Starr coming up with those glorious third-down passes to grind out the winning touchdown.

The losers—the guys who run around a football field all season long and fail to scale the heights—aren't the money players. If they were, they'd be the winners.

Who Needs Heidi?

New York Jets vs. Oakland Raiders—
November 17, 1968

Under ordinary circumstances a pro football game lasts about two and a half hours, give or take a few minutes. The elapsed time is figured from opening kickoff to final gun and includes time-outs, huddles, penalties, incompleted passes, conversion attempts, and quarter and halftime intermissions.

However, a great deal depends on the type of teams involved in the game, the weather, injuries, and dozens of other variable factors. For example, when two teams with strong running attacks face each other, the game doesn't last as long. A team such as the Green Bay Packers, under coach Vince Lombardi a few years back, played a ball-control game. They stuck to the ground most of the time, with Paul Hornung and Jim Taylor carrying the mail. It took time to get out of the huddle, run the play, untangle the tacklers and get back to the huddle again. All the while, the clock was running. Therefore, the Packers might run only three plays in a full minute, and a touchdown drive might eat up four or five minutes without the clock stopping.

A passing team is something else. The split end races out, and the quarterback throws the long one, but it doesn't make connections. So the end trots back to the huddle, and everyone waits; the clock is stopped. The play takes only five seconds to spin off, but it might be a full minute before another play begins.

A running-type game, overall, may take about two hours and ten minutes; the passing game might involve two hours and forty-five minutes.

Among those who make a science of figuring time down to the last split second are the television people. To those specialists, time is a valuable commodity, to be divided into one-minute commercials and twenty-second spot announcements. In order for the hard-sell messages to reach the ears of the public, the networks offer a variety of inducements: pro football, so dear to the hearts of male viewers, and fairy tales to keep the small fry spellbound. For Sunday, November 17, 1968, the National Broadcasting Company came up with a blockbuster of a schedule, guaranteed to keep the whole family happy.

During the afternoon, the men could plop into an easy chair before the "boob tube," open the first can of a six-pack, and watch "Broadway Joe" Namath and his New York Jets take on the big bad Oakland Raiders. Since Namath was already a full-fledged folk hero around New York and suburbs, the game guaranteed a soul-satisfying share of spectators for the network, at least in the crowded eastern part of the country.

To keep the youngsters watching after the game, NBC TV offered a remake of the old Johanna Spyri classic, *Heidi*. Everyone knows the sudsy tale of the little girl who goes to live with her surly old grandfather in the Swiss Alps, helps a lame girl walk and turns her grandpapa into a solid pillar of the community. Shirley Temple played the title role in the movies, and the television show featured a cute ten-year-old tyke named Jennifer Edwards; splendid Sir Michael Redgrave played the role of the grandfather.

Scheduling the time of both presentations was tricky. The computer-like minds of the television executives figured that both clubs had fine passers in Joe Namath and Daryle Lamonica (Oakland). It was obvious they would both throw the ball pretty often, and that might take up extra time. Okay. Figure three hours for the ballgame. There might be five or ten minutes left over, but television announcers were pretty resourceful, and the remaining minutes might be filled with a recapitulation of the highlights, maybe a few scores of other games, statistics, speculation on the future . . . that kind of thing. And there might even be time for another commercial.

The networks had a good thing going, for the Jets-Raiders game held more than passing interest all by itself. New York sported a 7 won, 2 lost record. For the first time since the American Football League was formed, the Jets had a clear shot at the Eastern Division championship. If they beat the Raiders, and if both Houston and Miami lost that day, the Jets were in. Oakland was in the thick of the fight for the Western championship. It figured to be a pier-six brawl from start to finish, and the Raiders were seven-point favorites.

Since the game was played on the West Coast, it was four o'clock in the afternoon when New York spectators saw the action begin. The Jets scored first, marching deep into Raider territory, and when things got sticky, Jim Turner booted a field goal from the 18.

Oakland retaliated quickly, chopping up the Jet defense with short passes and a good running game. To cap the drive, Lamonica tossed one to Warren Wells for the touchdown, and the conversion gave Oakland a temporary 7-3 lead.

Broadway Joe and the Jets fired right back with another sustained drive, and when the Oakland line held, Jim Turner swung his leg again for the 3-pointer. All that happened in the first quarter, and it ended with Oakland clinging to a 7-6 edge.

Even that early in the game it was apparent that this was going to be one of those penalty-filled donnybrooks. Both teams were "up" for the game, and tempers were bound to stretch thin. The officials, on the lookout for any slight infraction of the rules, were quick to slap on the penalties. Most of them were against the Jets.

In the second quarter, each team doubled its points. A Lamonica-to-Cannon pass, plus conversion, gave Oakland another seven points, while a Jet series culminated with Namath sneaking over from the 1-yard line on a keeper. However, when Joe tried for the equalizer with a 2-point conversion call, it misfired. The half ended with Oakland leading, 14-12. But that was practically no lead at all. With thirty minutes of football still to be played, and Namath firing the football with deadly precision, the Jets were sure to add some points. So was Oakland, on the strength of Lamonica's arm.

After the players had recharged their batteries at half-time, the clubs resumed hostilities, and the Jets forged ahead when Bill Mathis ran the ball over from 4 yards out. Namath went for the 1-pointer, and with Turner on the beam, that was almost automatic. The Jets were leading by 19-14 when the explosion came—and with it the turning point in the game.

Oakland had shoved its way to the New York 13. It was a third-and-5 situation, and the fired-up Jet defense was digging in. Lamonica called for a screen pass to running back Hewritt Dixon. He tossed a soft one out in the flat and Dixon caught it; but the Jets had smelled out the play, and Hudson came in fast to stop Dixon on the 11, which was 3 yards short of the first down.

As the Jets unpiled with grins of satisfaction, they were startled to hear whistles all over the field and flags being dropped at the spot where the tackle had been made. The officials were pointing at Hudson and indicating that he had been guilty of grabbing Dixon's face mask. And that was when the egg yolk fell into the air conditioner!

The New York defensive back lost his cool and began to scream like a wounded lion. He stormed, he ranted, he raved—and he began to cuss out the official, who turned on him with rage in his eyes and promptly ejected Hudson from the game.

That single play and what happened later have been discussed for many months. There have been conflicting stories aplenty, but the version agreed upon by most of the players involved, and those within earshot, was this:

Hudson had *not* grabbed Dixon's face mask. Even the Raider fullback admitted as much after the game was over. Hudson had gripped him with one arm under the chin, which was perfectly legal, and many pass receivers have been stopped far less gently. In fact Hudson had made sure he did nothing wrong because the Jets couldn't afford a penalty deep in their own territory. However, the official didn't see it that way.

Furthermore, when he threw Hudson out of the game, the official used curse words that would have made a truck driver envious of such an extensive purple vocabulary. Men have had their noses punched for far less. And that admission came from another Oakland player, who heard the whole thing from start to finish.

However, the Raiders weren't about to refuse such a magnificent gift. Not only did they keep the ball and get the automatic first down, but also that pesky Hudson, who had been bedeviling the Raiders all afternoon, was out of the game. In Hudson's place the Jets installed rookie Mike D'Amato, a willing but still green defensive back.

Oakland got the touchdown to lead, 20-19. And then Lamonica did some quick mental arithmetic to arrive at his next move.

If the Raiders added a 1-point conversion, they'd lead by two points. A Jet field goal would give New York the lead all over again. But if Oakland went for the 2-pointer and made it good, a Jet field goal could only tie the game. Thus a two-point lead wasn't as good as a three-point lead. And if the try missed, why, there was still plenty of time left; the Raiders would still be leading by one marker.

Lamonica flipped a pass, and it was good. The Raiders had their three-point margin, 22-19.

For a while it looked as if the Raiders would run up a big score against the Jets because, as the third period ended, they were knocking on the touchdown door again. But the first play of the new quarter turned everything around, and the next two plays after that left the Oakland bunch stunned.

This is how they went: Charlie Smith, the 200-pound halfback from Utah, tried to crack in and was hit so hard he fumbled. The Jets recovered on their own 3. Broadway Joe then hit flanker Don Maynard with a 47-yard heave, and then he came right back, firing a 50-yard rocket to Maynard for the touchdown. Boom-boom, and the Jets had a 26-22 lead!

Six minutes later the Jets tacked on 3 more points when Jim Turner kicked his third field goal of the day.

Daryle Lamonica rallied his club and sparked an 88-yard push to pay dirt, the score coming on a 22-yard aerial to his flanker, Fred Biletnikoff. The conversion tied it up at 29-all. This was indeed quite a ball game, and nobody was tuning out, even to get another beer.

Four minutes were left when the Jets took the kick-off. It was Broadway Joe's plan to play possession football, with just enough passes to loosen up the secondary. The passes did most of the damage, and Don Maynard, the lanky Texas flanker, was Namath's partner in crime. Joe hit Don with one pass good for 9 yards, then with another for 42. More yardage was picked up with a penalty when Ben Davidson, the 280-pound monster in the Oakland line, was caught roughing the passer.

The Raiders held fast, so the call went out for Jim Turner again. He came in, put one over the crossbar from the 18, and went back to the bench. It was his fourth field goal of the day. The Jets led, 32-29, and there were exactly sixty-five seconds left to play. Oh, this was turning out to be a nail-biter all the way down to the wire!

New York kicked off, and Charlie Smith returned the ball to Oakland's 23. Lamonica then reached Smith with a pass good for 20 yards, and another face mask call—the *fifth* of the day against the Jets—put the ball on New York's 43-yard line. There was something like forty-odd seconds left to play.

As the teams were returning to the line of scrimmage, the home screens suddenly went dark. What happened?

Time out? Possibly. Such things had been rigged in pro games, when sponsors realized that it was a good time to get in one extra commercial. Who'd leave the set at a time like that? But couldn't they wait just another minute?

The screens lit up again. There were the commercials. The viewers waited, muttering imprecations (and shouting them too). And then, instead of twenty-two dirty young men facing each other with do-or-die snarls on their lips, the TV audience saw the captivating image of ten-year-old Jennifer Edwards. As they stared incredulously, Johanna Spyri's 1880 classic began to unfold.

Undoubtedly, the roars of rage that followed weakened the walls of many a suburban and city living room. Later, NBC's New York headquarters reported that its switchboards lit up like Times Square on V-E Day as 10,000 calls overwhelmed the paralyzed, frightened telephone operators. Furthermore, outraged citizens were calling the police, calling local newspapers, calling anyone who had a phone, demanding to know what in blue blazes had happened.

And maybe it all happened for the best, for a benevolent fate decreed that no Jet rooter should die of a heart attack that evening. What took place in Oakland after the blackout of the game would surely have caused ambulances in New York to work overtime.

In the Oakland huddle, Charlie Smith told Daryle Lamonica that he could now get behind young Mike D'Amato easily enough and that it was time to run the fly pattern. That was the play Lamonica called. Smith charged out of the backfield, outran the befuddled rookie, took the pass, and went over unmolested. The Raiders led, 36-32.

But that wasn't all. On the ensuing kickoff, which

was a low, tricky shot, the Jets' Earl Christy was slapped down hard on the 12-yard line before he had full possession of the ball. Preston Ridlehuber picked up the loose football and rambled into the end zone to score the second Raider touchdown in nine seconds. Final score: Oakland 43, Jets 32.

Meanwhile, NBC was frantically trying to apologize and explain and soothe ruffled feathers. In desperation the network ran a streamer across the bottom of the screen during *Heidi*, giving the final score and imploring everyone to tune in the late news for further details. But that only added fuel to a fire that was already raging out of control! Where did those two Raider touchdowns come from? What happened?

All sorts of garbled information filtered out of the network offices. First, they tried to explain that a watch company had bought the *Heidi* show and paid for the time and was entitled to have it on the air. Then the nervous executives said that they wanted the game continued, but somehow there had been a "breakdown in interoffice communications." Somebody had failed to act on a telephone call from a top executive who made the decision. After that the statement was given out that the direct line to Oakland had been cut off when *Heidi* started and could not be restored. Pretty soon nobody knew which story was true.

Since that day, the television networks have a firm policy: *Never fool with a pro football game!* If it runs overtime, cancel the show that follows, or pick it up in the middle—"in progress." Because if a *Heidi*-type incident should ever arise again, those pro football nuts would undoubtedly organize a march on the studios and reduce the joint to rubble.

111

The Game

Yale vs. Harvard—
November 23, 1968

"Gentlemen, you are about to play a game of football against Harvard. Nothing that you do for the rest of your lives will be as important!"

Those words, spoken in a Yale locker room during a pregame pep talk by an Eli coach (some say it was Herman Hickman) were not mere rhetoric; the man meant every word, and the players believed him as though he were reading the gospel.

Only the rivalry between Army and Navy is as deep-rooted, as soul-filling. Yale and Harvard have been staging football battles since 1875, and when they clash, the stands are filled with a variety of old grads who religiously make the pilgrimage to New Haven or Cambridge. It has been said that unless an alumnus of these two schools is on his deathbed, or marooned in the Antarctic wastes, he will return to that contest like a swallow's annual homecoming to Capistrano. They come by train or by plane, and not a few in chauffeured limousines. Perhaps it is difficult for the average football fan to grasp the real meaning of a

Harvard-Yale set-to, but to the old timers it is crystal clear: this is The Game.

And when the real old-timers gather around, the names of the ancient football greats are reverently intoned: John Brown, Hamilton Fish, Charlie Brickley, and Ned Mahan of Harvard; "Pudge" Heffelfinger, Albie Booth, Clint Frank, and Larry Kelly of Eli Yale.

The 1968 game between the Cantabs and the Bulldogs held a special, deeper meaning than usual, for both clubs were undefeated and untied, and the winner would become champion of the Ivy League. By golly, The Game had real drama now! It had to be seen. Why, it just had to. The more elderly gaffers, unable to make the trip, had themselves cranked up in beds of pillows before their television sets, while nurses and physicians hovered nearby, holding flagons of adrenalin handy.

An analysis of the two teams showed the reason for their unblemished records. Harvard just had a good team, period. There were no all-Americans on the roster, but the defense was as solid as any in the East, and the running game was dependable.

Now Yale was just loaded with stars. Quarterback Brian Dowling could run and pass with the best in the country, while running back Calvin Hill was destined to be signed to a pro football contract with the Dallas Cowboys. Those two alone made Yale the pregame favorite. The experts were predicting a two-touchdown victory for Yale, and if Dowling and Hill got hot they might just turn the contest into a rout.

The Elis opened the scoring in the first period, moving down the field steadily, and Dowling went over from the 3 on a keeper. And in the second quarter the Bulldog offense continued to click, as Dowling tossed a 3-yard scoring strike to Carl Hill, and then a 5-yarder to Del Marting. One of the conversions was a 2-pointer, so Yale had a 22-0 lead in the second quarter.

Frank Champi, Harvard's quarterback, had a very strong arm. In fact, it was really not a football arm at all; Champi was a javelin thrower on the Crimson track team. Late in the second quarter he found the range with a 15-yard touchdown pass to Bruce Freeman; but the kick was blocked, and as the marching bands came out for halftime entertainment, Yale led, 22-6.

Harvard looked somewhat better in the third quarter. In fact, they didn't waste much time putting up seven more points on the board. The key play was a pass from Champi (who was actually the team's second-string passer) to Pete Varney, which took the ball to the edge of the Yale goal line. Gus Crim cracked in from less than a yard out. Now Harvard trailed, 22-13.

The Elis had been coasting comfortably; now the game was getting a little too close. The Blues drove 80 yards but lost the ball on a fumble. Frustrated, they stopped Harvard's thrusts, then came right back again to the Crimson 5-yard line. Dowling carried it across. The kick made it 29-13 as the last quarter got under way.

Twice Harvard got possession after holding Yale, and twice the Cantabs stayed where they were. It looked like a lost cause, especially when Dowling connected with a screen pass that carried to the Harvard 14. But then came one of the big turning points. When the Yale runner was dropped, he also dropped the football, and Harvard pounced on it.

That recovery seemed to spark the Cambridge guys, and they picked up steam. Only three minutes and thirty-four seconds remained on the clock when they began moving, and what happened after that will be talked about until both schools stop playing each other, which will probably be never.

Champi hit on a good-sized pass, and Yale was penalized. There was Harvard on the Eli 32. Champi tried another pass, but now the Yale line was ready and they red-dogged him all over the backfield. It's still not clear whether Champi fumbled or whether he tossed a lateral pass along the ground; in any case it was a free ball. Fritz Reed, a Harvard tackle who had played end the year before, scooped up the ball and fled to the Yale 15 before being downed. What had looked like a disaster turned out to be a 17-yard gain!

With less than a minute to go, Champi heaved one again, this time into the end zone. Bruce Freeman caught it. Touchdown! The teams lined up for the two-point conversion. Champi fed the ball to Gus Crim, who barreled in and dove over the chalk mark. And now it was 29-21, as the stands shook with stomping by gleeful Harvard rooters.

Everybody knew what was coming up next—the short, onside kick. The Cantabs had only one chance to pull the game out, but only if they got hold of the football. Yale anticipated that and sent in a few fairly good receivers instead of the burly tackles and guards who would normally line up along the 40-yard stripe. All they had to do was keep possession, run one or two slow line plays, and the ball game was locked up.

The kickoff was a love-tap, skittering over the turf. A Yale man got it—and fumbled! Harvard's Bill Kelly recovered on the Eli 49. Pandemonium broke loose in Cambridge! Crimson supporters pounded each other on the back while Yale men called for smelling salts. The

Cantabs were still alive, with just 42 seconds left on the clock.

The Yale line dug in, and the Yale secondary went into a kind of "prevent defense," hoping to keep any passes short ones while the forward wall blitzed in. Champi dropped back and scrambled all over the field, finally keeping the ball and running for his life. The Elis grabbed him and knocked him flat. But there was a personal foul involved against Yale which took the ball to the 35.

The Yale defense rose to shut off further gains through the air, and two passes by Champi were broken up. Sensing a weakness in the Blue's blitz, Champi called for a draw, and Crim went up the middle to the Yale 6-yard line as Crimson fans thundered and cheered and hollered.

Now Harvard lost 2 yards, and there were just four seconds to play. It had to be a pass; that was no secret. As the clock kept running, Champi dropped back again— and he was trapped. He ran backward and laterally while everyone in a blue uniform gave chase. Time had run out, but the play wasn't over yet, and nobody could hear himself think for all the uproar in the stands. And then Champi saw Vic Gatto standing all alone in the end zone. With a prayer he flung the ball away, and Gatto was there to catch it. Touchdown! Score: 29-27, Yale.

However, every team is entitled to a chance for the extra point, and Harvard certainly wanted that. The fans were down on the field ready to kiss the players, and it took a couple of minutes of pleading via the public address system so that the Crimson could have elbow room.

Once more Champi fell back into a pass pattern. Pete Varney, Harvard's split left end, curled over the goal line into the end zone. Champi saw him. The pass—the catch —the score!

THE GAME

The game ended in a 29-29 tie.

In a way it was fitting. For the first time in fifty-nine years the teams had gone into their classic game with unblemished records. Why should one of them have to lose? Especially when the Ivy League title was at stake.

Everyone had covered himself with glory. Brian Dowling, the crack Yale quarterback, had run for two touchdowns and passed for two more. Calvin Hill had scored a touchdown on a Dowling pass, and in so doing he passed the career scoring mark set by Yale's immortal Albie Booth. Frank Champi, Harvard's sub passer, had given Harvard grads something to talk about for the rest of their lives.

Some blasé folk think there is too much fuss and furor made over a football game and that there are more important things in life to think about. That's true enough. But sometimes a football game can have an extra special meaning which only those close to it can appreciate.

For example, take the rivalry between Tulsa and Houston. In 1967, these two teams clashed in their big game. Houston was ranked tenth in the nation, but Tulsa took care of their dreams with a nice upset victory. The Houston fans and players were stunned and vowed vengeance. They got it a year later.

The same day Harvard and Yale tussled, Houston took on Tulsa again, blood in their hearts and fire in their eyes. It was a slaughter. Final score, Houston 100, Tulsa 6!

Now that's *really* getting even!

The Super Bowl Story

Green Bay Packers vs. Kansas City Chiefs—
January 15, 1967;
Green Bay Packers vs. Oakland Raiders—
January 3, 1968;
New York Jets vs. Baltimore Colts—
January 12, 1969;
Kansas City Chiefs vs. Minnesota Vikings—
January 11, 1970

Traditionally, America is a land which dreams of full employment and equal opportunity. All men with a hammer and nails can become carpenters and rise to the exalted status of cabinetmakers. Give a man a brush and a pot of paint and in time he will become a Rembrandt. And if a young man in college can run with or throw a football, he has every right to expect that he will become a major leaguer.

Except that it doesn't always work out that way. Before 1960, there was only one major football league and that was the National Football League. There were just so many teams and a limited number of players per roster. Only the elite could join up. Besides, they weren't all that prosperous. Several NFL franchises were just about getting by, paying their bills for bandages and uniforms and saving what was left—if anything—for a rainy day.

Some promoters tried to form another "major league" back in 1946, and they called it the "All-America Conference." It lasted only until 1950, and then some teams were permitted to join the NFL intact, while others saw their players divided among the rest of the league.

In those days, pro football wasn't yet a gold mine. Some teams did all right, some didn't. The trouble was that not enough fans were familiar with the great brand of football show they put on. Sure, some cities had pro football heroes: Otto Graham and his all-winning play-mates were the demi-gods of Cleveland; Bob Waterfield, Norm Van Brocklin, and Tom Fears were almost as popular as Hollywood movie stars in Los Angeles; and Bobby Layne was darned near as well known in Detroit as Henry Ford. But how about Buffalo and Boston and Denver and some other big towns without major league football teams? What did they know about pro football? Where could people there see a game even if they wanted to?

The answer was television.

The Madison Avenue mob and the network geniuses discovered that pro football was just as violent as a cowboy or a gangster movie, and just as American, too. All they had to do was put these hulking brutes on the home screen and let the audiences gather round the sets. It was a mar-velous idea—and it worked!

Some wily money men, like Lamar Hunt of Texas, saw the potential riches to be gathered and decided to form another league. But it couldn't be a minor league organization. Nobody would bother with an inferior out-fit. Well, that was no problem; all they had to do was say it was a major league. This they did, but merely say-ing so didn't make it true immediately.

Basically, the new group didn't have the players. Few college stars would sign with the American Football

League in spite of the tempting offers dangled before them. Who knew how long the AFL would last? Better to do business with the old, established firms of the NFL. A few, such as Louisiana State's Billy Cannon and North Texas State's Abner Haynes, chose the new league, but most of the good draftees passed it by.

So the American League filled out its rosters with a lot of second-line players, NFL rejects, and over-the-hill veterans. True, a number of the castoffs had a lot of mileage left: George Blanda and Len Dawson couldn't cut it in the NFL, but they did pretty well in the new league. Rookie Lionel Taylor was dropped by the Chicago Bears, but that was their loss, because this guy was good, and he became as great a pass receiver as anyone over in the older organization.

So the AFL opened shop and played out a schedule. It seemed from the start that it was strictly a Mickey Mouse league. The offense took over and played a wide-open game; defense seemed to be a dirty word. Partly that was because it took time to weld a club into a unit, and these men had never played together before. Also—let's face it—the best tackles and ends and linebackers were in the NFL.

But with every passing year the league was building and enticing better players and coaches. The dreadful New York Titans lured Weeb Ewbank away from Baltimore, where he had produced a championship team, and new owner Sonny Werblin got a fresh supply of checks from his bank with which to buy some top college players. Everybody knows that he shelled out $400,000 for Joe Namath.

As the American League kept improving, it got cockier. A big network was televising the games over a national hookup, and fans had the option of watching one league or the other or both in action on the same day. The AFL began to wonder out loud whether or not it was as good as, or better than, that "other" league. There was only one way to find out, and that was via a playoff at the end of the year. Let the NFL champs take on the AFL champs, and that game would be the decider.

The National League wasn't about to get suckered into that kind of a deal, for it had everything to lose and nothing to gain. Suppose it clobbered the junior league? It would simply show that it was better, and that's all. Ah, but footballs take peculiar bounces; what if the AFL should spring an upset? How mortifying!

There were two factors that made the NFL change its mind. First was the price war between the two leagues. With television loot filling its coffers, the American League could sweeten the pot for any college star it went after and offer the same deal, or a better one, as might come from the senior circuit. Bonus prices went out of sight. Green Bay bought Donny Anderson and Jim Grabowski, and the combined price was *one million dollars!* An all-American who was offered a mere $100,000 to sign was insulted.

Furthermore, the signing machinations began to resemble spy movies. One team's representative would descend on a college star, fly him away in a private jet, and hide him out in some hotel, just so a representative from a team in the other league couldn't get to him with the sales pitch. When the fuzzy-cheeked footballer was comfortably settled in an easy chair, the inducements would begin, and they included new cars and post-season jobs and lots of money and pretty girls for dates and all sorts of goodies. Once the college guys had been worried about getting a C-minus in chemistry; now they had problems with taxes!

The second factor was the growing demand by the fans for exactly such a postseason game. Television sponsors, sensing the built-in audiences for that kind of "classic," readily agreed to foot the bill for the viewers. Television officials. tuned in to the sound of money, were quick to go along with the idea.

So, in 1966, the two leagues figured out a way to kill both ugly birds with the same stone. By merging into one league and holding a common player draft, the astronomical bonus prices would come down to reasonable levels. And that way they could play against each other without the stigma of one league losing to the other.

Of course, the merger would take time. It was not to be really effective until January 1, 1970. After that there would be realignment of clubs and dovetailing of schedules. In the meantime, league champs could play each other. It was only a temporary, four-year setup anyway.

Thus, on January 15, 1967, Green Bay, the titleholders of the National Football League, met Kansas City, the supreme team of the American Football League, in the first of what came to be known as the Super Bowl Games.

For the money players on the Green Bay team, this new postseason game was a delightful way to close out a year of playing football. Having taken the measure of Don Meredith and his Dallas Cowboys, they were already richer than other clubs in the NFL. Now there was more cash to be had: $15,000 guaranteed to each winner and $7,500 to each losing player. Except, of course, it was ridiculous to dream that they'd come out on the short end. The Pack just didn't lose the big money games.

The only thing Green Bay team members knew about Kansas City was what they read in the papers and saw in borrowed AFL game films. The films they could understand, because that was football, which could be analyzed and studied intensively. But the newspaper stories were something else.

For example, the Chiefs had a cornerback named Fred Williamson who proclaimed himself a very tough egg and threatened to do dreadful things to Green Bay receivers with his secret weapon, which he called "the hammer." Supposedly, the hammer was his forearm, which he brought down on the head of the receiver with a karate-chop motion. During his pro career, said Williamson, he had busted apart thirty helmets on the heads of luckless pass catchers.

Now what kind of talk was that, coming from a full-grown adult? Who was he trying to scare? Certainly not the Pack, because they thought it was wildly funny. During practice sessions they loped around the field calling out to each other, "Hey, look out! I'm the Hammer, and I'm coming to get you!"

There were several other players on the Kansas City Club who were not so funny, and Green Bay did some serious thinking about them. Defensive tackle Buck Buchanan was a six-foot, seven-inch brute who threw his 290 pounds around with reckless abandon. Many times he had rattled the molars of a running back trying to go up the middle against the Chiefs. Mike Garrett, the all-American from the University of Southern California, was only a little guy, but how he could fly! He was the American League's answer to Gale Sayers of the Chicago Bears. Quarterback Len Dawson had won the AFL passing championship three times, and a mediocre passer just can't do that. Fred Arbanas was the equal of any tight end in the NFL, and one look at the game films proved that conclusively.

Still, the Packers weren't worried. They were heavy favorites, and only the most optimistic, die-hard Kansas City fans would dare dream of a possible upset.

For half a game the Chiefs gave the Packers all the trouble they could handle. Very early in the game wide receiver Boyd Dowler was injured, and he was replaced by the older and slower Max McGee.

Green Bay got going first. Max McGee gave defensive back Willie Mitchell a fake with the shoulders and a nod of the head, and breezed right by him to take Bart Starr's 37-yard touchdown pass. But Dawson got that one back when he lobbed a 7-yarder to fullback Curtis McClinton.

The Packers went ahead again in the second quarter after a drive capped by hard-nosed Jim Taylor's 14-yard dash. Back marched the Chiefs, and when they couldn't go all the way, Mike Mercer settled for 3 points from the 31-yard line. It was very much a tight ballgame as the teams took a halftime breather. Green Bay had a surprisingly small 14-10 lead.

Vince Lombardi had been coaching for a long time, and he knew what his boys had to do in order to shut off the KC offense: stop playing careful football and open up. Start blitzing in on Dawson. The Pack wasn't noted for its red-dogging of quarterbacks, although they got to the passer often enough during the course of a game. Now they had to adjust. They did.

Once again the Packers did the job on the strength of a single defensive play!

Kansas City was moving well. They had the ball on their own 49, third and 5 to go. Obviously a pass was coming up.

The play Dawson called in the huddle had the two backfielders move to the right, so that free safety Willie Wood had to move over to cover at least one of them. Meanwhile, tight end Fred Arbanas went to the left on a sideline pattern. A fairly short one to Arbanas would pick up the needed yardage and keep the Kansas City attack going.

All afternoon the Packers had not blitzed in on Dawson. Now they did when he wasn't expecting any such move. Startled, he hurried the throw, even before Arbanas had turned his head to look in the passer's direction. Willie Wood raced in, picked off the throw and sped down the sideline. Only a tremendous sprint by Mike Garrett stopped him from going all the way. He didn't have to, because Elijah Pitts did it for him later. So the Packers had an 11-point spread, and now the Chiefs had to play catch-up football.

They got nowhere. The Pack scored again in the third quarter on another Starr-to-McGee pass, and once more in the final period on a plunge by Pitts. The final score was 35-10. The money players from Green Bay had done it again!

Now it was 1968. The Super Bowl scene had shifted to Miami, Florida. The American League challengers were the Oakland Raiders. But one thing remained the same, and that was the National League entry: still the team from Green Bay, Wisconsin.

Oakland had chopped up the American League in

awesome fashion during the regular season, compiling a 13 won, 1 lost record. Their defensive line was shored up by two walking brick walls named Ben Davidson and Ike Lassiter. Davidson rose six feet seven inches into the stratosphere and weighed in at a dainty 270 pounds. Lassiter weighed as much but was two inches shorter. Rumor had it that they ate quarterbacks as though they were fried chickens, with each taking a leg for a drumstick and an arm for a wing. And linebacker Dan Connors was no sissy either.

The attack was nicely balanced. Quarterback Daryle Lamonica was among pro football's better pitchers, and he had able catchers in Bill Miller, Fred Biletnikoff, Warren Wells and a few other worthies. Hewritt Dixon and Pete Banaszak took care of the running game in fine fashion. They were pretty light, but both boys were fast and shifty.

In spite of that good lineup and the imposing record, few experts gave Oakland much of a chance. After all, they had won thirteen games against American League teams, and what did that amount to? Was there a club as good as Dallas in the AFL? No. As formidable as the Los Angeles Rams? Of course not! So whom did the Raiders beat? Just the other AFL humpty-dumpties, that's all.

And the Packers set out to establish their superiority right away. They kicked off because Oakland won the toss, and the Raiders returned the ball to the 28.

On the first series of plays, Hewritt Dixon tried to probe the Green Bay line, and was belted hard by middle linebacker Ray Nitschke. No gain on the play. Next, Lamonica tried a square out pass to Fred Biletnikoff; Herb

Adderly knocked the ball out of the receiver's hands. Another pass to Dixon was too low. So after three plays there was no gain. Oakland punted to the Green Bay 34. The Pack started its ball control attack and pushed ahead over the chalk stripes until they reached a point just short of the Raider 30. When the attack sputtered, Chandler place-kicked the ball and gave Green Bay 3 points. That took eleven plays. And the field goal accounted for all the scoring in the first period.

Lombardi's stalwarts went back to work in the second quarter, and this time they really had a long way to go, because a Raider punt sailed out of bounds on the Green Bay 3-yard line. But Starr kept gnawing away until his teammates had reached the Raider 13. There they stopped. Chandler trotted out with the kicking tee. When he went back to the bench, the score was 6-0.

Oakland still could not put together any kind of attack, and after the punt, Green Bay had the ball on its own 38. The Raider defense tightened up, expecting either the line smash or the quickie flip. But Bart Starr, that old fox, flimflammed them immediately. He sent Boyd Dowler scampering long and hung one out to him on the run. Dowler never broke stride as the 62-yard touchdown play unreeled. Now it was 13-0.

When Oakland got the football again they managed to put it all together. In nine plays they were on the board, the touchdown coming on a 23-yard heave to Bill Miller. That made the score a respectable 13-7. And it showed that the Raiders could indeed move the ball when everybody did his job properly.

Furthermore, the defense didn't permit Green Bay to take its usual liberties after the kickoff. The Pack punted.

Roger Bird signaled for a fair catch. The Green Bay men slowed up, and Bird promptly dropped the ball. Green Bay recovered equally as promptly.

There wasn't much time left, and Starr had to hurry. Two passes missed connections, and the third one gained 9 yards. With just one second remaining, Don Chandler limbered up briefly, went out on the field and kicked a very nice 43-yarder. So it was 16-7 at the half.

Much has been said and written about Vince Lombardi's type of slow, steady, grind-it-out type of ball-control attack. There were those who said it wasn't worth the effort. A touchdown that took five minutes to attain could be equalized by one long bomb, and then the Packers would have to do it all over again. Lombardi didn't see it that way, obviously. He operated on the sound principle that the other guys couldn't score when his guys had possession of the football. And an analysis of the next Packer touchdown showed how the plan worked.

Green Bay had the ball on its own 17. Starr handed off to fullback Ben Wilson, who went up the middle to the 31. Next, Donny Anderson cracked over the left side for 8 yards, and Wilson bucked into the center for another yard. Needing just a couple of feet for the first down and noting the tightened Oakland line, Starr faked a handoff to Wilson and threw to old pro Max McGee, who made it all the way to the Raider 25. A pass failed and a draw play gained only a yard. On the third-and-9 situation, Starr sent Carroll Dale on a slant-out pattern and caught him with a pass for the first down on the 13. A pass to Donny Anderson failed because Donny dropped the ball. Starr came right back to Anderson with another pass, and this time he held on for the first down on Oakland's 2-yard line. Anderson messed up the next play when he bumped into Starr during the handoff. Once more Starr called Anderson's number; finally the kid bored into the end zone.

So—eleven plays, 83 yards, and 6 points. Don Chandler's kick didn't really count as another play. Score: Green Bay 23, Oakland 7.

Two seconds before the third quarter was history, Don Chandler kicked his fourth field goal from the 31. That boot almost didn't make it. The ball hit the crossbar and bounced over. It was a sloppy 3 points, but Green Bay wasn't particular about how they scored—just as long as the scorekeeper kept the totals correctly.

Down by 19 points, the Raiders pushed the panic button and Lamonica began throwing long. He had nothing to lose by going to the bomb. If the Raiders were going out, it wouldn't be because they didn't try to come back at least part way. Tight end Billy Cannon ran a diagonal toward the sidelines, and Fred Biletnikoff's pattern was a simple turn-in toward the middle. Lamonica hoped to sucker Adderly into committing himself on either one and then going to the other receiver. But Adderly knew what was coming and he simply waited while Willie Davis lumbered in on the passer. Lamonica threw toward the sideline; Adderly cut in, grabbed the ball, and streaked away. He picked up two key blocks on the 10- and 5-yard lines and had himself a 60-yard touchdown. Score: 33-7.

The Raiders did score again before the gun sounded, and it was on another 23-yard pass to Miller. After that the football season was over, except for a couple of all-pro games here and there.

The experts nodded their heads wisely and made their snide remarks. Same old Green Bay money players, same old American League patsies. The Pack scored 2 points less than last year, and the AFL entry had 4 points more than Kansas City, so maybe the new league was improved by a total of 6 points.

How could anyone know that better days were coming?

The 1969 Super Bowl produced a brand new cast of characters. No longer were the Green Bay Packers a part of the action.

Perhaps it was because they had all grown old suddenly. Or maybe they lost out because Vince Lombardi was no longer around to snap the whip and snarl and goad them to victory. Lombardi had retreated to a front office job and turned the coaching reins over to his chief assistant, Phil Bengston.

The Baltimore Colts were on hand to defend the honor and fair name of the National Football League. How they got there was a Horatio Alger story of the first order.

Before the season began, the Colts acquired veteran quarterback Earl Morrall from the New York Giants. Morrall was one of the most-traded players in the NFL, and it appeared that he had reached a dead end in his career. There was no future in hanging around as backup man behind Johnny Unitas, and Morrall was ready to call it quits. Coach Don Shula persuaded him to stick it out for just one more year. Luckily for Shula, Morrall agreed.

Then disaster struck. Before the season started, Johnny U's arm was injured, and he couldn't lift the limb even shoulder high. Nor could treatment bring the arm back to life. It just hung like a pendulum with fingers.

Into the gap stepped Earl Morrall, who had never amounted to much before. He was considered a very ordinary journeyman passer, adequate but not quite good enough to rate with the best. Yet the battle-scarred veteran led the Colts to one of their greatest seasons ever, a 13-1 record. Only the Cleveland Browns had beaten them, and in the postseason playoffs Baltimore had mangled the Browns, 34-0.

Representing the other league were Joe Namath and his rowdy gang of New York Jets.

When Paul "Golden Boy" Hornung cast aside his shoulder pads for the last time, the title of pro football's swingin'est star was inherited by the lean quarterback from Beaver Falls, Pennsylvania. He spent his bonus money where it showed up best, and that included a thick white llama rug in his East Side apartment and the biggest automobile ever manufactured (some jolly wits said that the only way to park that car was with the aid of a land-going tugboat); and at his side were some of the curviest chicks ever to slip into a tight miniskirt.

What Namath did off the field was one thing; when it came to playing football, he was all business and no pleasure. Joe Willie had guided the Jets to a very healthy 11-3 won-lost record. Two of the losses had been upsets at the hands of Buffalo and Denver, real weak sisters. The other defeat had been that wild *Heidi* game, a loss the Jets had avenged by knocking off the Raiders in the play-offs to win the AFL championship.

The Jets' coach also provided an interesting story. Weeb Ewbank had been Baltimore's coach before taking the same job with the Jets. He had fashioned the Colts into a championship team, which wasn't so hard consider-ing he started out by having Johnny Unitas as his passer. Now, with Joe Namath—who, he said, would become as good as Unitas someday—Ewbank had taken an American League title. He was the only coach who could make a claim to two leagues and two championships.

But it was Namath who got all the headlines. Reporters followed him everywhere and duly wrote down every word he uttered. Joe Willie couldn't hide his puckish streak, and he began to needle the Colts, using the newspapers as his means of communication. Baltimore wasn't really that good, Joe said; Oakland had a better team; Morrall was just a lucky guy enjoying a fabulous hot streak; there were a couple of passers in the AFL who were infinitely better. The Baltimore front four of Bubba Smith, Billy Ray Smith, Ordell Braase, and Fred Miller were inferior to the Kansas City defensive line, said Joe; he wasn't afraid of them.

It was hard to tell when Joe was kidding and when he wasn't. He had the same deadpan expression and the same twinkle in his eye no matter what he said. And so when Namath *guaranteed* that the Jets would win, few took him seriously. Should he have predicted a Baltimore victory? Now wouldn't *that* be a vote of confidence in his own team!

New York was a decided underdog, with the spread ranging from 17 to 21 points. Most "experts" thought the best they could hope for was a respectable showing, say a two-touchdown loss. The majority made it plain they thought Baltimore so much better that the slaughter might be worse than any inflicted by Green Bay in the two previous games. Only one sportswriter smelled an upset and that was Stan Isaacs of *Newsday*. But he wasn't about to guarantee anything. It was just a hunch.

The most confident player of all was Baltimore's defensive end, Bubba Smith. Standing six-feet-seven and weighing 295, Bubba looked like a giant redwood tree, except that he could move—and fast. In spite of his size, he could "get off the ball" quicker than men fifty and sixty pounds lighter. He had the reflexes of a cobra and the strength of a bull elephant. Bubba noted that Namath set up for a pass much deeper than other quarterbacks; that kept the defense farther away from his multi-scarred knees. But that didn't matter to Bubba. The Colts were bound to reach him sooner or later, and then Joe Willie would find out what it meant to get hit. Furthermore, Jet receivers had never experienced coverage like what they would get from the Baltimore secondary.

If Namath heard Bubba, he was too busy to reply. For he and his henchmen had abandoned the cuties for a while and were studying films of Colt games. What they saw was quite surprising.

All season long Baltimore had used the safety blitz with deadly results. But there was a flaw in the execution, and after repeated viewings, Joe spotted it.

Just before the safety blitz was sprung, the Colt safety man crept in three, four, even five steps, so that he was quite close to the line. If the enemy quarterback spotted him and called an audible to change the play, the safety man retreated. If no audible was called, he went barreling in.

So, Joe reasoned astutely, there were two ways to handle the Colt safety blitz:

First, call a *fake* audible. Make it sound like you're changing the play, but don't really do it. That would send the safety man back where he came from.

Second, don't call any play at all in the huddle. Just gather around in a circle and say nothing. Call the play at the line of scrimmage. The safety man would hear no audible being called, and he'd come running in. Then pass into the spot he left open.

Yet it looked too simple to be right. If Namath had spotted that weakness so easily, why hadn't all the geniuses in the NFL seen it over a fourteen-week schedule? Was everybody in the other league blind? Hardly likely.

Joe Willie and his buddies kept looking for other weaknesses, and they found a couple of others. Their names were lineman Ordell Braase and linebacker Don Shinnick. By comparison with others in the defense, they looked slower, less sure of their tackles, more easily shoved aside.

To sum up, it seemed to be possible to run against the right side of the Baltimore defense. And, if their deductions were right, a Colt safety blitz would play right into Joe Willie's hand.

It took a while, though, before Namath could find out whether he was right or wrong. Fortunately for the Jets, that interval left no scoring scars.

Baltimore missed one golden opportunity and then another. Early in the game they moved to a first down on the Jet 19 where New York held. Lou Michaels, ordinarily a dead-eye Dick, missed an easy field goal.

Before New York could get going they were in a jam again. Namath found George Sauer with a pass, but Lenny Lyles hit the receiver so hard that he fumbled. Ron Porter recovered for Baltimore on the Jet 12.

Two plays picked up 5 yards, and on third down Morrall called for a pass to Tom Mitchell. The throw was on target all right, but it was too soon and too hard. Mitchell had barely turned around to look for the ball when it bounced off his shoulder pads and into the eager arms of defensive back Randy Beverly, who grounded the ball for a touchback. Instead of leading by 10, the Colts had nothing.

Now it was time for Joe Willie Namath to put his theories to the test. He began by handing off to Matt Snell, the hard-running fullback. It was the type of running play that left the direction of the plunge entirely up to Snell. If he felt like hitting the center hole, he could; or he could go over his right side or the left side. Snell chose to move into the right side of Baltimore's defense, where Braase and Shinnick were stationed.

Four straight times Matt Snell bucked over that area, and he accumulated 26 yards in the process! Namath was right after all.

The Jet quarterback nursed the drive along. He missed on one pass but hit on all the rest: to Bill Mathis on a flare for 6, to Sauer for 14, to Sauer again for 11. Emerson Boozer ran for a couple of yards, and then Joe Willie went back upstairs with a quickie to Matt Snell for a dozen more yards down to the Colt 9. Then it was Snell pounding the right side for 5, and Snell again in the same place for 4 yards and the touchdown.

Namath and Snell had combined to make Brasse and Shinnick look like tired old men. In the second half they would be benched in favor of Lou Michaels and Ron Porter.

Meanwhile, Morrall wasn't moving the team at all. Nervous, puzzled, he abandoned the short-pass game in an effort to put the Colts on the scoreboard, and that was precisely what he shouldn't have done. In fact he hit on only five of fifteen attempts in that first half.

One of the last attempts before intermission was a real desperation play—the Baltimore "flea flicker." Morrall handed off to Tom Matte, who ran wide, stopped and threw a lateral back to Morrall. The crazy play might have worked, because Jimmy Orr was all alone just a couple of yards from the end zone; but Morrall didn't see him. Instead he threw the ball into a crowd of players, with Jerry Hill as his intended target. Jim Hudson got there first with the interception to blunt the attack.

In the third quarter coach Don Shula reached into his bag of magic and played his big trick; he sent Johnny Unitas in to replace Earl Morrall. Sore elbow and all, Johnny U did his best. A handoff to Tom Matte produced the longest run of the game, a 57-yard broken field trip to the 16 of New York. And then Unitas suffered the same fate as Morrall: an interception. Johnny Sample, a Baltimore castoff, took the ball away from Willie Richardson.

During the third stanza Namath engineered two more drives, each resulting in a Jim Turner field goal. One of the marches almost came a cropper: a Namath pass was nearly intercepted by Jerry Logan, but Logan dropped the ball.

In the fourth quarter Turner got his third field goal of the day, and then the handwriting was on the wall. Baltimore couldn't come back. They might score—and they did—but it was too little, too late. Even after the touchdown and conversion were posted, and Baltimore tried the onside kick and got the football, everyone knew the Colts were finished, done, kaput.

The lowly, despised American Leaguers had finally done it. The final tally was 16 for the Jets and 7 for the Colts.

What was it that defeated a strong Baltimore club? Interceptions hurt. Four Baltimore passes fell into the wrong hands, while Joe Namath had a clean slate. Missed passes didn't help. Twice the usually reliable John Mackey dropped the ball when it hit him right on the fists. Once a pass misfired because the quarterback threw too hard from too short a distance. That cost the team a touchdown.

Two missed field goals by Lou Michaels subtracted 6 possible points. He had made tougher kicks from more difficult angles in the past. In the Super Bowl game they didn't go over the crossbar.

And Joe Namath's ability to read a defense could not be overlooked. He detected a weakness on Baltimore's right side, and it was a cakewalk for his fullback. He spotted the giveaway of the safety blitz; the Colts blitzed five times, and four of those times Namath threw to the gaping hole behind the line because he saw the safety man coming in.

And so the third Super Bowl game went into the record books. The National League led in games won, 2-1, but there was still one more to be played.

A lot of knowledgeable people firmly believed that Joe Namath was star-kissed and that somehow he would lead the Jets to the AFL title again. They were wrong; Kansas City was on top at the end of the playoffs.

Those same knowledgeable people also believed that Baltimore couldn't possibly repeat, because Johnny U was over the hill and the running attack couldn't pick up the slack. They were right; the Minnesota Vikings became NFL champs.

In any number of ways the two ball clubs were remarkably similar. Each boasted the biggest and strongest front four in the entire National Football League.

Minnesota rooters lovingly dubbed the defensive line "the Purple People Eaters," and they looked the part, too. Among them the beefy quartet totaled half a ton—a thousand pounds of walking destruction. During the season they had busted through to the quarterback forty-nine times, or an average of about three-and-a-half times per game. To run against them was suicide. To hold on to the football while they were storming in was sheer madness. Their names were Carl Eller, Jim Marshall, Alan Page, and Gary Larsen.

The Kansas City forward wall did not have a fancy nickname and didn't particularly want one. But they were just as heavy, just as big and equally as strong as the Four Norsemen. The Chiefs' front four had been only slightly less effective when it came to dumping the passer, for they accomplished the trick forty-eight times. They also gave ground grudgingly against running attacks. Reading from end to end they were Jerry Mays, Buck Buchanan, Curly Culp and Aaron Brown.

Neither team seemed particularly strong at the quarterback position. The Chiefs had stuck with Len Dawson for many years, and he was still around, although he had lost much of his former mobility. Dawson was accurate and steady, but he seldom threw long; that diminished his effectiveness, for the cornerbacks and safety men could shorten up on him in anticipation of the short ones. However, Dawson had the advantage of coach Hank Stram's very tricky offense, which included the I formation, the T formation, and a setup called the "movable pocket." Dawson would take the snap and roll out behind the line, right or left. This took him away from half of a possible blitz by the opposition's defenders. Most of the time it worked pretty well.

THE SUPER BOWL STORY

In form and style, Minnesota's Joe Kapp looked like the worst quarterback in all of football, pro or college. He seemed to do everything wrong. All other passers gripped the ball at the laces; he took hold of the ball anywhere at all and sent it on its way. He threw off the wrong foot. He threw off balance. All other quarterbacks would rather swim in shark-infested seas than try running the ball; Kapp loved nothing better than to leave the pocket and run directly at an incoming linebacker. He weighed about 190 pounds with all his toenails unclipped, yet he never hesitated to knock heads with a player twenty and thirty pounds heavier. So how come the Vikings were champs with such a chump for a passer? Because somehow Joe Kapp, the refugee from Canadian football, managed to get the job done. He was one tough cookie.

So it figured to be pretty much of a defensive game, and the Chiefs had a slightly better defense against passes. But the difference wasn't that noticeable.

Minnesota took the kickoff and traveled from its own 20 to the K.C. 39 before the Chiefs applied the brakes. Instead of going for the field goal, the Vikings elected to punt. That wasn't a vote of no-confidence in place-kicker Fred Cox. There happened to be a gusty fifteen-mile-an-hour wind blowing, and a 46- or 47-yard attempt looked like a bad investment, especially that early in the game. So Minnesota punted and the Chiefs took over on their own 17.

In eight plays Kansas City was on the Viking 41, but six of those efforts were window dressing. The two that counted were a 17-yard pass to Mike Garrett and a 20-yard aerial to Frank Pitts. Jan Stenerud came in to try a place-kick from the 48 and he made it. But then, he had the wind at his back.

139

Minnesota went through an unrewarding series of plays and kicked the ball over to the Chiefs, who started trying from their own 20. Once again there were two plays that ate up the yardage: a 20-yard pass to Frank Pitts, the wide receiver, and an interference call against Minny's Ed Sharockman on the 32-yard line. The Chiefs picked up another few yards, and when all else failed, Stenerud repeated. This time he had to kick against the wind, but 32 yards wasn't that far and he made it.

So far neither team had done much damage, and both goal lines appeared undentable. Joe Kapp tried to break through and almost did when he hit Johnny Henderson, but there was a fumble immediately after the catch, and Johnny Robinson recovered for K.C. Dawson fared little better as his high floater was picked off by Minnesota's Paul Krause on the Viking 7.

The next time Kansas City gained the football, the team managed to squeeze down to the Viking 17, and the People Eaters stopped the attack again. It was Stenerud from the 25. Score: 9-0, Jan Stenerud leading the Vikings.

Finally the break came. The kickoff sailed out to Charlie West, who tried to find the handle and couldn't. Before he could take firm possession, Remi Prudhomme covered the ball with his body on the Viking 19-yard line.

Minnesota's huge Four Norsemen got down on their hands and knees and tried to hold off the fired-up Chiefs. They defied the K.C. running backs to try going through on the ground. Throughout the season, Minnesota's forward wall had yielded only three touchdowns rushing, a formidable record indeed.

It took six plays to crack in. On the last one, 260-pound guard Mo Moorman pulled out and practically wiped out the entire right side of the Minnesota line as Mike Garrett followed close behind. K.C. went into the dressing room leading by 16-0.

The teams resumed slugging it out almost immediately after the second half kickoff. The Viking defense was solid and the Chiefs had to punt out. Joe Kapp took over and became a man possessed of devils. He ran for 17 yards and passed to Johnny Beasley for 15 more. Bill Brown traveled for 11 on a screen pass, and Oscar Reed reeled off 12 additional yards. The touchdown came when Dave Osborn busted over right tackle, broke away from a man who was clutching at his legs and fell over the last chalk stripe. Now it was 16-7.

There was no fire in the hearts of the Chiefs as they roared back—simply sound, pick-the-defense-apart football. Dawson had noticed that the Viking Norsemen moved in a set pattern: the two ends pinched in from the sides while the guards came on straight ahead. Twice they had fooled Carl Eller by going around him, using Frank Pitts on an end-around run. They did it a third time, picking up an important first down.

The big play came after that. Flanker Otis Taylor lined up against cornerback Earsell Mackbee, and when the ball was snapped he took two or three quick steps as if he intended to run right by the whole Viking secondary. Mackbee was forced to drop back to keep himself between Taylor and open country. Only Taylor stopped short and came back, wide open. Dawson fed him the ball and Taylor turned to make his dash. Mackbee came in fast and hit the receiver a solid shot, but the powerful flanker shook it off as if a gnat was buzzing his kneecaps. As Taylor sped goalward, safety man Karl Kassulke slanted over to stop him. Taylor faked once, twice, swiveled his hips, and left Kassulke empty handed. The play covered 46 yards. Now it was 23-7.

Still Joe Kapp refused to believe the Vikings were a beaten team. He had to be convinced forcibly, and the no-nickname Kansas City foursome did just that. As tough Joe dropped back to throw one, Jerry Mays thundered in at him and stripped away the pass pocket. Kapp ran to his left, hotly pursued by Aaron Brown. When Kapp turned for a last look to see if anybody was open, Brown piled in and dropped him flat. When Joe Kapp got up he was holding his stringy arm tenderly; it was a shoulder separation. Kapp was through—and so were the favored Minnesota Vikings. The score didn't change after Otis Taylor's dash.

So in four Super Bowl games the once lowly American League had gained an even split. It had taken ten years to get rid of the newness, the stiffness, the amateurish appearance of the league, but it had been accomplished.

And the Super Bowl, as such, was a thing of the past. Oh, they might call it by that name when the kings of the American Division and the National Division got together, but it would be in name only. Now both leagues were just one big happy family.

Were the Super Bowl games really "great moments in football"? Yes, but only in the sense that *all* championship games are great, have a built-in air of excitement, a tension. Otherwise they weren't in the least spectacular. But then again, of all the thousands and thousands of pro and college games that have been played, how many can be called truly great?